CHILDREN'S OBJECT LESSON SERMONS
BASED ON THE
COMMON LECTIONARY YEAR C

CHILDREN'S OBJECT LESSON SERMONS

Jim and Doris Morentz

Based on the
Common Lectionary Year C

Abingdon Press • Nashville

CHILDREN'S OBJECT LESSON SERMONS
BASED ON THE COMMON LECTIONARY YEAR C

Copyright © 1985 by Abingdon Press

Library of Congress Cataloging in Publication Data

MORENTZ, JIM.
    Children's object lesson sermons.
    1. Children's sermons. 2. Christian education—
    Audio-visual aids.   I. Morentz, Doris, 1929-
    II. Title.
    BV4315.M6273   1985   252'.53   84-28468

ISBN 0-687-06498-8

Scripture quotations unless otherwise noted are from the Revised
Standard Version of the Bible, copyright 1946, 1952, 1971, and ©
1973 by the Division of Christian Education of the National
Council of Churches in the U.S.A., and are used by permission.

MANUFACTURED BY THE PARTHENON PRESS AT
NASHVILLE, TENNESSEE, UNITED STATES OF AMERICA

To
Jim and Deb—who taught us everything we know
about children, especially the joys of being parents.
And to
our grandchildren—who taught us what only grand-
parents know—it is different the second time around.
Emily, who came from Korea in September 1979, and
Andy, born February 1980, children of Jim; and
Christopher, born to Deb in September 1983.
And
to the good Lord who has let us live to see all this
happen.

Contents

Introduction

Children seem to mature faster and get smarter each year. In the previous two books, for Years A and B, we tried to elevate the children, not talk down to them. This book, Year C, goes a bit further in this process. In testing these children's sermons, the children seemed to have stayed right with us. I hope you find this true. If you do, we both have succeeded in our goal to interest and elevate the children's part of the service.

Notice!

In the Year B book we suggested you have a person take on the job of putting together all the objects, series by series. It is a year-round treasure hunt. We have heard from many of you that you did this and what a joy it was to walk into the office and have a box filled with all the objects for the next series. We suggest you copy the list at the beginning of each series, pass it along to your dependable treasure hunter, and sit back and enjoy. To us, finding the objects for the sermons has always been the biggest nuisance of children's sermons. No more. Try it, you'll like it!

Suggestions on
How to Use This Book

We wish we could tell you that every one of these sermons will be fun to present as well as educational and interesting. If we could assure you of that, it would mean we were perfect in our preparation and you were perfect in your presentation. We worked hard on our end; if you work hard in the preparation and presentation on your end you should do well. You must study what we have to offer, get comfortable with it, and do it your way. Consider us a resource, not a word-for-word presenter.

The church year is divided into seasons. Some of the longer seasons are divided into several series. An introduction to each series explains the theme and lists the objects required. If you took our suggestion and found some treasure hunters, you could give them the lists of objects for the whole year. You might even want to buy them their own book so they can understand the use of the objects.

Relax and enjoy; it will show.

Advent

(*Four Sundays*)

This series should be a fun series. It is based on the sights and signs of an approaching Christmas. It builds during these four Sundays to the excitement of Christmas. There is a basic assumption that a mall is in or near your community. If there is none, you will have to substitute the local shopping center. Help build the anticipation and excitement of the children as Christmas nears.

Objects Required
- ☆ string of Christmas tree lights
- ☆ record of Christmas carols
- ☆ two Christmas cards—one religious; one with Santa Claus
- ☆ branch from a Christmas tree

First Sunday of Advent

Gospel Lesson: Luke 21:25-36
Key Word: **Near**
Object: Christmas tree lights

I was in a mall the other day and what do you think I saw? It was decorated for Christmas with lights all over the place. Here is a string of Christmas lights that one day soon will be on my Christmas tree. The malls always seem to get a head start on everyone else. I wonder if they do that because they are so excited about Jesus coming, or if it is just good for business? For whatever reason, at least they are the first to announce that Christmas is *near*. That is our key word for this first Sunday of the Advent season. For the four Sundays of Advent we will be talking about the signs of Christmas. The decorated mall is surely one of the early signs of Christmas.

I said our key word already. Who can remember what it is? That is right—near. Do you know what the word "near" means? It means "a short distance or close." That certainly is what Christmas is now. It is getting so close, just a month away. I am really getting excited. How about you, boys and girls? I have my Christmas lights right here. (Hold up a tangled string of lights.) If I start now I may have them all untangled in time for Christmas. Sometimes I think the same people who make the toys that say "easy to assemble," are the same ones who invented strings of Christmas lights.

There are a lot of other signs that Christmas is getting near. Can you tell me anything that has happened already? We had a big parade, that is right, and there have been some television specials. It seems as if everybody has a TV special for Christmas. I think it is a little strange that everyone is getting ready for Christmas except Luke, the writer of our Gospel lesson for today. Luke is talking about Jesus telling his disciples about the end of the world. He is telling them how men will be judged, how we should be afraid. That certainly slows down and kills some of the excitement of Christmas. Let me remind you that today is also New Year's Day in the church. Don't you think it is a good way to be reminded that every year also has an end to it? That is the message of this lesson. Years and lives have ends to them, be ready. Hold on now, boys and girls, I don't want to end on such a down note. We started out so happy, there simply must be something to get us back in the mood for Christmas. Oh, look at this! Verse 29, "Look at the fig trees . . . as soon as they come out in leaf, you see for yourselves and know that the summer is already near." Jesus is telling us there are signs for every season. The leaves on the trees come out in summer; it gets cool in winter; even the end of the world has its own signs. We have signs too, not the kind that Jesus knew about. There was no electricity then, so they did not have Christmas tree lights. The signs of Christmas are all around us. The parade, the TV specials, the Christmas lights, and, yes, even, and especially, the Christ Child. For some people all the glitter and rush of Christmas may hide the Christ Child, but not from us. Boys and girls, we will never let anything get in the way of the real meaning of Advent, in our church. The Christ Child is near. Get ready for his coming.

Second Sunday of Advent

Gospel Lesson: Luke 3:1-6
Key Word: **Crying**
Object: Christmas carols (record album)

What word in our Gospel lesson means "to call loudly or shout"? Does anyone know? Crying! When most of us hear the word *crying* we think of a baby lying in a crib, trying to get some attention—big tears running down the baby's face. When we think of crying, we think of tears. No tears, no crying. If you think about the definition I just gave you, it is what we all do when we cry. We call loudly or shout. You do not always have to have tears. In our Gospel lesson for this second Sunday of

Advent, we find John the Baptist, "the voice of one crying in the wilderness." Our word today is *crying*.

Guess where I was again this week? I was at the mall. It is beautifully decorated for Christmas. If you have not been there, you must go to see it. I was wandering around, just looking about, when all of a sudden I had a strange feeling that someone was trying to get my attention. I looked around and saw many people, but no one I knew. I went on with my wandering when, again I had this strange feeling, someone trying to get my attention. I stopped and looked around, really good this time, I still could not see anyone I knew or anyone who seemed to know me. It was a little spooky. Then I began to laugh to myself. Do you know what it was? (Hold up record.) It was Christmas music. With all those people around me, rushing here and there, all busy, busy, busy; arms full of packages, rush, rush, rush. Most of them were in such a hurry they never even looked up, just in one store and then another. Right in the middle of all this hubbub I heard the Christmas carols! Like a voice crying in the wilderness of the mall I heard, "O, little town of Bethlehem, how still we see thee lie." Isn't that weird? The carols were crying out the good news of Christmas and the whole mall was too busy to hear or pay attention to what that message was. I thought about how John the Baptist must have felt, out in the wilderness, crying out to all the people, but no one would listen. I tried something right there in the mall. I sat down on one of the benches, closed my eyes, and tried to blot out everything that was going on around me. Sure enough, after a little bit, something came through very clear. This time it was, "Joy to the world! the Lord is come." The message was very clear, it was me and my busy mind that was cluttered up.

If you stop and sit and listen for the sounds of Christmas, they are there. That is exactly why we have Advent. To give us a chance to get ready for the arrival of the baby Jesus on Christmas Day. I have wondered sometimes why Advent is four weeks long. Now I know, it takes that long for the message to get through to some of us. John preached and baptized out in the wilderness, and so few listened. More and more we hear the music of Christmas, in the mall, on the radio and TV, all around us, but we don't hear the message. Try something for me today. Go home and put on some Christmas music, play it, but listen to the words. Block out everything but that message. It is Advent. Get ready. There is a voice crying in the world today, Joy to the world, the Lord has come.

Third Sunday of Advent

Gospel Lesson: Luke 3:7-18
Key Word: **Winnowing**
Objects: A religious Christmas card; a card with Santa Claus on it

Have you ever played with a sifter or a piece of screen at the beach? You toss the sand at the sifter or screen and the clean sand goes through the little holes and the stones fall in front of the screen or stay in the sifter. Some of you may have been in the kitchen when Mother decided to perform one of her miracles—mothers do perform miracles, once in a while. They take out eggs, butter, salt, baking powder, milk, sugar, four ounces of baking chocolate, and flour. Did you hear that, chocolate? Then they put all the dry ingredients in the sifter and sift until everything is smooth. The other things are added and all mixed together and put in a pan ready for the oven. Now here is the miracle; the pan of mix going into the oven will turn into a big, delicious-looking chocolate cake. Oh, Mom, how about a miracle today? I was so caught up in sifting sand and making a cake I forgot how I started. "To sort out, separate, sift." That is what our word for today means. The word is one we do not use much any more, but it is a good one to know. It is *winnowing*. Today, when farmers cut their grain fields they have big fancy combines that cut the grain. It separates the grain from the stalk and blows the grain out the back and into a trailer, ready to go to the storage bins. In the days of John the Baptist, the farmers waited for a nice windy day, and using big forks they would throw the newly cut grain up in the air as far as they could.

The light stems blew away and the grain fell to the ground. That was called winnowing; to sort or separate the good from the bad. To get things perfect you have to refine them. That is what John is telling us in the Gospel. Stand back, take a look at your life, see if you can make it a little more perfect. Do not just say I am pretty good, that may not be good enough for God, he wants you really good. Someday he will come to separate all that is perfect from all that is useless.

I almost forgot to tell you that it is still Advent. Just a few more weeks until Christmas. Is everyone excited? (Take the two Christmas cards and give them to two children.) All right, hold up what I just gave you so everyone can see. Now tell me what it is. Yes, a Christmas card. Both of them are Christmas cards. There is a difference, however, between the two cards. Can anyone see what the difference is? This one is a religious Christmas card; the other is just a Christmas card. If you got either one of them in the mail they would say to you that someone was thinking about you. This one, the religious card, also has the message of Christmas. The baby is lying in the manger. God is sending his son. That is the real message of Advent and Christmas. Prepare the way, baby Jesus is coming. It is always nice to think of people, it is even better if you send them the right message.

Fourth Sunday of Advent

Gospel Lesson: Luke 1:39-55
Key Word: **Living**
Object: A branch from a Christmas tree

Whenever a woman is going to have a baby she always sees only the best and brightest future for her child. You never hear a mother say, "I think my child will grow up to be a bum," or "I think mine will spend most of his life in jail." Never. Mothers always have the highest hopes for their children. These two mothers-to-be, Elizabeth and Mary, are overjoyed at the prospect of having their babies. These are not just two ordinary women. They have had a visit from an angel who told them about the miracle that is about to happen to them. If an angel told you that you were going to have a baby, I think you could be pretty certain that child would have a good chance of becoming a success. In our Gospel today we have two beautiful witnesses by these two women, one very young and one very old. In spite of all the high hopes these two mothers had for their children, we know that neither one of the children lived to be thirty-five years old, and both died as (what the world would call) failures. I guess it is good that parents do not know what the future of their children will be or we would be scared to death, either by their success or their failure. Elizabeth and Mary knew something very special was in store for their two children, but they did not know what it was, and that was a good thing.

The Gospel lessons in Advent jump all around, but they have a common theme that runs through the season leading to Christmas. Get ready, the baby is coming. This Advent we have had Jesus preaching, the Old Testament prophecy of the Lord's coming, John the Baptist preaching, and now we go back to before John and Jesus were even born. All those events are leading us right to Christmas. Our word today does not appear in the Gospel lesson, but it is all through it. The word is *living*. I have here a branch from a Christmas tree. Next week we will have a big, live tree here in the church. Do you see that this branch is from a live tree? Many people that I know have artificial Christmas trees. I guess they dress them up like live trees, but that's like the two Christmas cards from last week—a nice thought, but it does not deliver the right message. Advent is the time, at the beginning of the church year, when we announce to the whole world that a child was born in Bethlehem, who came to change the people of the whole world. Get that message right. Santa Claus does not bring that message, aluminum Christmas trees do not bring that message. The message is: He is alive. The message is that as these two mothers talked about the future, they were sure that their sons would make a big difference in the world. They both died as very young men, they both died as failures. They both live today, because God's plan will be fulfilled, not because of people, but in spite of people. This is the end of Advent. Now we are ready for Christmas. I would like to invite all of the children to a birthday party at our Christmas service.

Christmas Eve
or Christmas Day

Christmas Day or Christmas Eve services are usually long. The children need their own spot. The success of this sermon will depend on the cooperation of the organist and choir to make it happen the right way. When you talk about a children's Christmas carol, no one will think of *Happy Birthday, Jesus!* in the middle of a church service, but trust me, it works. After you say the words, the organ and choir must come in, joined by the children the first time and everyone the second time. Try it, you will love it and so will everyone else.

Objects Required
☆ Christmas decorations

The Nativity of Our Lord

Gospel Lesson: Luke 2:1-20
Key Word: **Carol**
Object: Church Christmas decorations

This is a big service, so the children's sermon will be a little shorter than usual, but it is a great one. I have two questions for you. One is our word for today. What is a *carol?* You know, like a Christmas carol? It is a song of joy. That is what this service is all about, a service of joy, so we sing Christmas carols, songs of joy. Second, why do we have the church decorated? Look at the beautiful flowers and the extra candles. Even the choir is bigger. The church is filled with people, that is always good to see. What is happening?—it is Christmas. But what is Christmas? It is Jesus' birthday. What kind of a birthday party would it be without some decorations? If we are going to have a birthday party, we need five things. Decorations, we have them. Gifts, we will give those to Jesus in a while through our offerings. We need cake and ice cream, but we do not have them at this party. We need to sing happy birthday to the birthday child. That we can do. This is our own children's Christmas carol to the Christ Child. Our own song of joy. Even our organist knows this carol. Mothers and fathers and all the rest can join us, we won't be selfish on a day like today. Let us all sing that grand old carol, "Happy Birthday to you, Happy Birthday to you, Happy Birthday, dear Jesus, Happy Birthday to you!" Have a blessed Christmas.

Two Sundays Following Christmas

These two Sundays are a time for you to let your hair down a little. Let the kids in on the fact that you have to prepare each sermon, it does not come as an inspiration from on high. The kids will enjoy the inside information, and the adults may learn something also. You may be amazed how many adults ask after the service "What did you say that book was you used today?" It would be helpful to show them how long the Gospel lesson is in the Bible and how long the commentary explanation is for the same verses.

Objects Required
☆ Bible
☆ commentary

First Sunday after Christmas

Gospel Lesson: Luke 2:41-52
Key Word: **Understanding**
Object: A Bible

I hope you had a great Christmas; we did at our house. Now we come to the Sundays after Christmas. There are usually two Sundays after Christmas. Today our word is one that is at the bottom line of every sermon I ever preach, whether it is a sermon from up in the pulpit or down here with you young people. The bottom line in every sermon is *understanding*. That is our word for today, *understanding*. If, when I finish a children's sermon, you do not understand the message, then I failed. When you are in school and the teacher says, I am going to teach you something new today, and you do not understand what it was she taught you, then she failed. Kids end up in fights, friendships are broken, sometimes forever, just because someone did not understand what another person was saying. Countries go to war because they do not understand the needs of each other. On Easter, Jesus died on the cross, not because he was a bad man, but because the people did not understand what he was saying.

Understanding what is said and what is meant is so important. How many times, when your mom or dad were angry with you, did they say, "I just don't understand you"? In our Gospel lesson we see that the leaders of the Temple gathered around this twelve-year-old, and they were amazed at his understanding. The reason they were amazed was they did not understand to whom they were talking. After three days, when his mother found him (you can imagine if you were lost from home for three days how upset everyone would be), Mary could not understand how her son, Jesus, could do this to her. What a better world this would be if there were a lot more understanding.

Boys and girls, what do you think Jesus was talking about to the leaders of the Temple for three whole days? The Bible. That is our object for today. (Hold up Bible.) Now I am going to let

24

you in on some secrets about how I go about preparing a sermon for Sunday morning. Please, don't let this get out to all the rest of the people in the church, this is just between us kids, OK? Before I start to prepare a sermon, I read the Gospel lesson in this Bible. Then I read a few verses before and after the lesson so I have a better understanding of what is being said. This is a very important part of understanding. What happened to this person before and what may happen next. If your mother has a headache, and she is upset with you, you can understand it better if you know what is going on with her. I hope that since you have been listening to my sermons for a while, you may have suspected that the first place I start in preparing sermons is the Bible. Because I went to the seminary does not mean I know all the answers. Just like you, I did not go to get all the answers so that I would understand everything, I went to find out how to find the answers to questions. That is how I try to understand more each week, by looking for the answers to my questions, and then telling you so we can understand one another and all the messages and answers that can be found in this book. My first place to turn for understanding, the Bible. Next Sunday we will share another secret.

Second Sunday after Christmas

Gospel Lesson: John 1:1-18
Key Word: **Through**
Object: A commentary

Remember last Sunday I told you my first secret about preparing a sermon? This week we have a bigger secret. Here is a book I use all the time. It is like a road map for me after I read my Bible, remember that is where I said I always start. Sometimes, after I read the Bible, I still need some help to get a picture of what the message from the scripture is saying. I then turn to this book (hold up commentary). This is called a commentary. Explained in great detail is the meaning of each verse in the Bible. It refers back to the Old Testament verses where the New Testament is a fulfillment of these verses. It also gives the background on what you are reading, this can be helpful as you try to understand.

I will not embarrass any of you by asking you to explain the Gospel lesson for today. What I am going to do is to tell you a little of what I found out as I read this commentary. It is very interesting. The Gospel lesson for today is John 1:1-18; these eighteen verses are like an introduction to what the book of John has to say to us. John is giving us a review of history. He tells us, in the review, that in the beginning was God, God made the world, and the world was in darkness. God sent John the Baptist to tell us about the new light that was to come. The new light was Jesus, who came, and we did not accept him. God, through his son Jesus, was God among us. Through Jesus we received grace. Now here is the big one, verse 17, "For the law was given through Moses; grace and truth came through Jesus Christ." That is a summary of all time, right up to John's time. This is the introduction to John's Gospel. That is what I discovered in this commentary—all the background you need to understand. It is like an encyclopedia you use at school. It has all sorts of information to help you understand what you read. Our word for today wraps up this entire message. The word is *through*. That word was mentioned about five times in our lesson today. It means "because of." It was used in front of the word for God or Jesus. If we understand what "through" means it adds to the message. I will finish by just changing the last of the "throughs" in the lesson, and it will help us understand. Ready? This is part of verse 17 again, "Grace and truth came through (or because of) Jesus Christ," and that is the truth.

Epiphany

Epiphany (January 6) is not a special service in most churches. In case you are one of those churches, here is a children's sermon just for you.

Object Required
☆ a pillow

Eight Sundays after Epiphany
Since Christmas has just passed, we will do the Epiphany season with a model train set. The train set seems to make a logical bridge between Christmas and Lent. Using various cars and combinations of cars to illustrate the Gospel should fascinate the young people and hold their interest.

Objects Required
☆ engine   ☆ refrigerator car
☆ dining car   ☆ passenger car
☆ station   ☆ passenger car and caboose
☆ caboose   (log or crane car)
                  ☆ engine and caboose

Transfiguration
(Last Sunday after Epiphany)
This is a one-Sunday series. With a little simple magic we will transform some water right in front of everyone. Simple to do, but a very effective and fun demonstration.

Objects Required
☆ two glasses of water
☆ food coloring—yellow, red, blue, in dropper bottles

The Epiphany of Our Lord

Gospel Lesson: Matthew 2:1-12
Key Word: **Mother**
Object: Pillow

This is a story we have heard year after year on Epiphany. A story of the three wise men. When you listen to our Gospel lesson for today, it is possible to miss the message of the lesson, and I think the message is so special for all the children. I have here a nice, soft pillow. Who went to bed a little late last night and had a tough time getting up this morning? All right, you, here is a job for today's sermon. Take this pillow, find a spot and put it on the floor, lie down and rest while we have the rest of our lesson. Relax, take it easy. I will keep an eye on you so no one will bother you. Trust me, you do a good job of resting, and if I ever need another person to lie down on the job, I will call on you. Oh, by the way, you don't snore do you? Good. Now for our story. We have seen Christmas cards with pictures of the three wise men on them. There is a star in the sky with rays coming down. The men are usually on camels. That is the way rich persons traveled in those days. They had servants leading the camels. Then we see other pictures of the wise men laying their gifts in front of the manger, with Joseph and Mary standing and watching. King Herod asked the three distinguished guests to come back and let him know where the baby was so he could go and worship him. He really wanted to kill Jesus. In a dream, God told the three wise men not to go back to Herod but to go home another way. The three wise men did as they were told, and they were gone from the Bible and out of history forever. Can you imagine that here in the Gospel lesson, in twelve verses, they came and went and we still have Christmas cards and pictures about these three men? This is a very beautiful story. It seems to be a Christmas story even though it happened on January sixth. What are a few weeks among friends? Now that we know the story we come to the question we like to ask in these children's sermons. What special message does this story have for us today? You, back there, don't go to sleep, we are coming to your part in the service. Here is the special message for all of us. God will look out for you every day of your life just as he did for his own son. Here comes our big part for our sleepyhead back there. Put your head on the pillow, just like you do when you are getting ready to go to bed at night. I think every kid has a routine they go through when it is time to go to bed. First, you brush your teeth, put on your pajamas, hop into bed, often someone reads you a story or you read your own, then it is prayer time. Mom tucks in the blankets, fluffs up the pillow, and tells you to sleep tight, she will be close by. You shut your eyes and know you are safe. You asked God to take care of you, and he will, but Mom and Dad are there too, just for a little extra protection. That is the real message of the three wise men. Not the gifts, but that for the first time in the Bible we see God step in and say, I will keep my son safe from harm. If he will do it for his son, he will do it for you. Sleep safe and sound, God takes care of all his children. (Turn to the one on the pillow.) "Take up thy pillow and walk."

The Baptism of Our Lord
(First Sunday after Epiphany)

Gospel Lesson: Luke 3:15-17, 21-22
Key Word: **Expectation**
Object: Engine

I don't know when a set of electric trains became a part of Christmas. At some time in their lives every boy has had a set of trains. Now even girls have them. I suspect the reason we see so many sets at Christmas time is that fathers like to play with them, too. Now God understands that Dad likes trains, he doesn't mind. He also likes to keep fathers humble; he has a way to fix trains so they never work on Christmas Eve. After much fussing and fuming, God says, Let them run. It happens every year. We have a set of trains we will be talking about during this

Epiphany season. Instead of putting them away for another year we will use them a few more weeks.

Here is our first part of the train. (Hold up the engine.) Who can tell me what this is? An engine, that's right. The engine is the first part of the train, so it is only proper it should be the first part of our series. There is something different about this part of the train than the others. Can you tell me what it is? Right, this has a motor. It pulls the whole train, it supplies all the power to make the train move. No other part of the train can do that. Some cars may have a motor to do a little job, like the crane car has a motor to move the crane, a tank car has a motor to run the pump that empties the tank, but only the engine has a motor big enough to pull the whole train. Look at the engine I have here. This engine has no power to pull a train full of cars. Let me tell you something about engines. There are three different kinds of engines, they all do the same thing, just in different ways. There are steam engines, electric engines, and diesel engines. One runs on coal and steam, one on electricity, and one on oil. You can have a powerful engine that is able to pull one hundred and fifty cars loaded with food, coal, cattle, oil, wood, automobiles, all going to market. But this powerful engine cannot pull anything; in fact, it can't even move itself because it is not connected to its source of power. It needs electricity, or oil, or coal and water. Then it will be a great powerful engine, until then it is only a great big piece of useless steel.

Today is called the Baptism of Our Lord. This is the day Jesus was in the wilderness listening to John the Baptist preach and baptize. Jesus watched all that was happening and then stepped forward to John and said, "Now I am ready for the power." Jesus was baptized and the power flowed into him. He was strong enough to pull the whole world after him. Then as proof of this new power, God said, "Thou art my beloved Son; with thee I am well pleased." The power was in the engine, the journey was about to start. Our word today is *expectation*. The people expected something to happen. It did, but most of the people missed it. There were no miracles that you could see, just that Jesus now had the power to change the world, and he did.

Second Sunday after Epiphany

Gospel Lesson: John 2:1-11
Key Word: **Wedding**
Object: Dining car

I have a lot of questions to ask you today. First I will ask all the questions, then we will talk about them. How many of you have ever been to a *wedding?* Good, just about all of you. How many of you have ever ridden on a train? Not too many. How many of you have ever been to a party? Everyone, that is good. Today in the Gospel reading there are two big lessons. I don't want you to miss either one of them. Jesus performed the first miracle of his ministry. Can you imagine having 120 gallons of water turned into wine? That really was a miracle. The reason Jesus did this at the wedding was because the host was very embarrassed about running out of wine. Jesus felt sorry for him and helped him out with this first miracle. That is the first lesson. The second thing I don't want you to miss is that Jesus was at a party. It was a wedding party. A fun time. Everyone has fun at a wedding and later at the party. So many people forget that Jesus was human. He was a lot of fun. He went to parties. He liked to laugh. When he was a young boy, he played games with the other children in town. He was a fun-type person. People liked to be around him. We have talked about two of our questions, weddings and parties. Now how about the question of trains. I think that before too long we won't be able to take a train ride, there will be only freight trains. About fifty years ago trains were the way to get around. Now we have buses, airplanes, and automobiles. If we were going to take a train ride, a long train ride, what do you think would be your favorite car on the whole train? (You will get several answers, just say, That would be fun.) Let me tell you my favorite. The dining car. (Hold up a dining car.) This is where you have all the fun. The party car. If you have never eaten in a dining car rolling through the countryside you don't know what you've missed. I do not know whether the food is better on the train, or if it just tastes better.

Some of these cars even have a piano with a person who plays soft music while you eat. I even knew of one that had a three-person band on it. That was a real party. Do you know that a train, in one day, can go farther than Jesus traveled in his whole lifetime? That is how small the world was in Jesus' day, and how big it is today, with all the new ways to travel. Let us go back to the Gospel lesson. Remember, Jesus performed his first miracle at a wedding party. Jesus was a nice man who loved a good time, who was human. Don't ever forget, as you travel through life, Jesus was the kind of person you would like to have as a friend. He still is. He is my friend. I hope he is yours also.

Third Sunday after Epiphany

Gospel Lesson: Luke 4:14-21
Key Word: **Home**
Object: Station

Do you know what we have today from our train set that will show you what the Gospel lesson is all about? It is the station. Now what do you think a station has to do with our Gospel for today? A pretty tough question. Jesus went to the synagogue to read the scripture and to speak. A synagogue is the same as a church, but they did something a little different there than we do here. When they read from the Bible they stood up. When they spoke, like when our ministers preach, they sat down. This was to show the difference between God's word and the word of the person speaking. Jesus went to the synagogue to read and speak. Do you remember where the synagogue was located? The Gospel gave us the name of the town. Remember, it was Nazareth. What was so special about Jesus going to the synagogue in Nazareth? He was born there.

I have this station because Jesus is coming home. It was an exciting time for Jesus and all his family. Remember, he had brothers and sisters. The whole family came to see him. A real family reunion. I can just hear some of his relatives saying to one another that, "He does some pretty strange things," and hoping he doesn't embarrass them in their hometown. He disagrees with the priests and leaders of the synagogue. It sure would be nice if he could just cool it and behave. He comes back here and upsets everybody and then takes off. We have to still live here. I guess I should tell you, at this point, that Jesus came home after he was in the wilderness, when for days and days he was tempted and tried by the devil. He had come through all that and now returned home. In the wilderness Jesus found out who he was, what his mission on earth was all about, and he was ready to come home to start his ministry. If his relatives had known what a mood he was in, they would have run to this station and taken a train out of town until Jesus had left Nazareth. He came *home,* our word for today. A place where you should feel safe, surrounded by friends and family.

Let us see how Jesus' homecoming worked out. He went to the synagogue and all his family gathered there, so proud of him. He picked up a scroll and read from Isaiah 61. I will read it to you because you have to hear it and just imagine you were there that day, one of Jesus' relatives. As he started to read, his relatives remembered the passage from today's Gospel lesson, they were certain he couldn't get in any trouble with that.

> "The spirit of the Lord is upon me,
> because he has anointed me to
>   preach good news to the poor.
> He has sent me to proclaim release
>   to the captives
>   and recovering of sight to the blind,
> to set at liberty those who are oppressed,
> to proclaim the acceptable year of the Lord."
>   Luke 4:18-19

He closed the book and gave it back to the attendant, and sat down. All the people in the synagogue were looking at him. His relatives were pleased, they hoped he wouldn't say anything else. Then Jesus said, "Today this scripture has been fulfilled in

33

your hearing." He said, "I am the Messiah. The one the scripture is talking about." His relatives could have just died! He seems to make some crazy statement everywhere he goes. Stay tuned, next week it gets worse.

Fourth Sunday after Epiphany

Gospel Lesson: Luke 4:21-30
Key Word: **Acceptable**
Object: Caboose

Did you ever have one of those days when everything went wrong? I mean everything. You woke up late, you could not get your hair to stay down. Mom had forgotten to buy your favorite cereal. You missed the school bus, and Mom had to drive you to school. You had worked long and late last night to finish a special project that was due today. When you got out of the car, all the other kids in your class were carrying their projects, and then you realized you didn't have yours. Your mother agreed to go and get it and bring it into your schoolroom. Everyone walked into the room with their projects, except you. Then, just before the class began there was a knock on the door and there was your mom with the project. All eyes are on you, the kids are making fun of you since your mom had to bring in your project, she had to save you. Won't you ever grow up? Now that is a bad day. Let me tell you about a day Jesus had when he went to visit his hometown. Remember last week, we had a station to show that Jesus came home again. This week we have a car that will give you some idea of the day Jesus had. When you see that big, old freight train going down the tracks away from you, what is the last car you see? Yes, the caboose. As we watch the caboose disappear, it gets smaller and smaller until it is finally all gone. The chances are good that the caboose will be at the end of that freight train when it comes back, tomorrow or next week or whenever, but it will come back someday. When Jesus' caboose left Nazareth, it never did come back. Jesus had such a bad day in Nazareth that he never, ever, came home again. Remember how we imagined we were Jesus' relatives, worrying about Jesus starting something while he was visiting his hometown? Last week he started out harmless enough with Isaiah 61, then ended up saying he was the one Isaiah was predicting would come. His relatives thought he had gotten himself and them in all kinds of trouble; he was just warming up. "No prophet is acceptable in his own country." That is saying, don't get upset at what I am saying, I did not expect you to understand. Then, as if that was not bad enough, he tells them that all the great prophets had the same trouble; Elijah and Elisha, God sent them, and no one listened. When they heard him use the names of these great and beloved Old Testament prophets, and say all three of them had the same problem, no one listened to him, they had had enough. He was escorted out of town. They took him past a big, high cliff. Their plan was to throw him over the cliff, but Jesus ducked, got away from the mob, and went down to Galilee. That is what I call a bad day. It is sort of sad, isn't it that Jesus never went home again?

Fifth Sunday after Epiphany

Gospel Lesson: Luke 5:1-11
Key Word: **Toiled**
Object: Refrigerator car

Do you ever get the feeling that you are the unluckiest person in the whole world? I guess all of us feel that way once in a while. You play in Little League baseball. All season long, you get a lot of hits and never make an error. Your grandparents come for a visit and go to one of your games. You guessed it, no hits, many errors.

You're going on vacation; you've waited and waited for the big day. It has been so hot at home. You guessed it again, it rains and rains during your vacation. Everyone tells you, You should have been here last week.

You and your father plan a fishing trip. You have all the gear ready, a nice lunch and plenty of soda. The day arrives, and it is beautiful. After fishing for eight hours all you have is two little fish, a bad case of sunburn, and an upset stomach. It must have been the food you ate. You return the boat and the man at the dock says, "Any luck?" You show him your two little fish and he says, "You should have been here yesterday."

"We have toiled all night and took nothing." That is what Peter told Jesus when he asked about the fishing. Our word for today is *toiled,* a word we do not use much anymore. It means "worked." Peter worked hard all night and caught nothing. All Peter needed was to have this preacher come along and tell him how and where to catch fish. I have a hard time believing that Peter, who had a temper, didn't lash out at Jesus, and tell him, "Look, preacher, you preach, I'll fish." Hard to figure out why fishermen won't listen to preachers' advice.

Peter and his partners were tired, they were ready to go home to get some sleep. Then they thought maybe Jesus did say some things that made sense, why not try again? They shoved off to sea again and soon had fish. I mean they had fish! Their friends came over to help out, they each filled their boats until they almost sank. Peter was really scared. He had not only a temper, he was also very excitable. As a fisherman, Peter knew that there were no fish out there. Not one. Now his boat was almost sinking with so many fish. What will he do with all the fish? In Peter's day you had to sell the fish right away or they would go bad quickly. Here is our train car for today. This is a refrigerator car. Today the fish would just be frozen and put in a car like this and they could be sent anywhere in the whole country. It is the same old story, Peter should be here today. We know how to handle all those fish. Here was Peter with the biggest catch of his life. He has the chance to make a great deal of money. Suddenly Peter forgot about his big catch, and all the money he could make, because he realized that he was in the presence of a great man. Jesus said, "Do not be afraid, from now on you will be catching men." Peter did not understand what was happening. He looked at Jesus and followed him along with his two partners, James and John. No one will say to you, "You should have been here last week," you are here just in time for the invitation of Jesus to follow him.

36

Sixth Sunday after Epiphany

Gospel Lesson: Luke 6:17-26
Key Words: **Blessed** and **woe**
Object: Passenger car

Did you notice that our lesson for today has four "blesseds" and four "woes" in it? I think that is a nice balance. For every blessed there is a woe. Do you have any idea what *blessed* means? It means "enjoying the favor of heaven." You are in pretty good with God. *Woe* means "you are in trouble." I think sometimes we feel we are one of the woes. I am certain this has happened to each and every one of us at some time in our lives. Let us say it is your birthday and a big party has been arranged. There will be fifteen of your friends at the party. You surely will be getting some nice presents. Everything is set. The birthday cake, ice cream, special hats and napkins, and even decorations.

Everyone arrives and the party starts. You receive many nice gifts, games are played, and you even won one of the prizes. You are one of the blessed. Hold it now. We are not done. Here comes the ice cream and cake. You really enjoy it. Two pieces of cake, lots of candy, and ice cream. It is the greatest party ever. When it is over, and everyone has left, your mother asks you if you had a good time. You agree it was the best time of your life. This is what blessed must mean. About an hour later something strange happens to you. You have the biggest bellyache you have ever had. You are so sick you are afraid you will die. This must be what woe is. Woe, the opposite of blessed. Our words today are *blessed* and *woe*. This little birthday story shows us that we can be blessed and also have woe, if we are not careful. Here is our train car for today. It is a passenger car. The passenger car on a train is a lot like the four blesseds and the four woes in our lesson. There are first-class cars and coaches. The coach cars are like the blessed and the first-class cars more like the woes. Just like the birthday party. Sometimes we think we are the happiest, and suddenly we have a problem that just ruins our whole day. Jesus is not saying it is bad to have money. What he is saying, if you are in first class, do not ever forget the rest of the world, those riding in coach, the poor, and hungry. The blessed are not blessed because they are poor, but because they know they need God. The woes are not woes because they are rich. They are woes because they forget the poor and think they do not need God. One final word about our first-class and coach passenger cars. Rich or poor, when you look out the window, you both see the same world go by. What does your eye see as the world goes by you?

Seventh Sunday after Epiphany

Gospel Lesson: Luke 6:27-38
Key Word: **Choose**
Objects: Passenger car and the caboose (log or crane car)

Our key word is not in the lesson today, but it is all through the lesson in one way or another. Our word is *choose*. Life seems to be full of choices. We seem to be surrounded by a world that says choose. When we got up this morning the first thing we had to do was choose what clothes to wear. Then, what we want for breakfast. What are we going to do after church? Do you have any homework? When are you going to do that? Are we going to stay for church school? What kind of sandwich do you want for lunch? What time do you want to eat? Life seems to be full of things to choose.

We have been using a train set for our objects during this Epiphany season. Even this brings choices to be made. Do we have passenger cars or freight? Here is a passenger car, and here is a caboose from a freight train. You can have only one set, which will you choose? I bet most of you would pick the freight set. Do you know why? There is more to do with a freight set. There are so many cars in a freight set (hold up a log car or crane car). With the passenger cars you can stop at the station and pretend to let people off. The freight cars really work.

I am so involved with the train sets I almost forgot our Gospel lesson for today. I told you before that life is full of choices. Let me explain a little. Most of my friends are people whom I like, that is why they are my friends. If one of them does something I do not like, that is all right. I will forgive them. One little thing will not break up our friendship. That is the real test of friendship. Jesus asks, can you get mad at each other and then be friends again? Certainly. Anyone can forgive a friend when the friend wrongs you. How you choose to treat someone you do not like when they have done something to you is the question. Love your enemy, give him the shirt off your back; if he hits you, let him hit you again, don't fight back. If you do something good for a person, don't expect them to do the same for you. If you lend some money, don't expect to be paid back. Do you have any idea, if you would choose to live like that, what the kids at school would say about you? They would think you were some kind of nut. Do you think I expect you to be that kind of person? I sure do. You have to choose? That is what Jesus is asking us to do in this lesson. Not what kind of train will you have, but what kind of life will you choose? Be different. Choose a life of love and forgiveness. That is how Jesus wants us to choose.

Eighth Sunday after Epiphany

Gospel Lesson: Luke 6:39-49
Key Word: **Lead**
Objects: Engine and caboose

This is the last Sunday with our set of trains. What do you think would be a good car to use for this last Sunday? Right, the caboose. The only trouble is we used the caboose a couple of weeks ago. Instead of using just the caboose, I decided to use the caboose and the engine. I think it is very interesting that no one lives in the engine, but they do live in the caboose. It is like a little house on wheels. There are a kitchen and bath and something to sleep on. In spite of all this, it cannot go anywhere without the help of the engine. The engine is always the leader. It is the power and the eyes of the whole train.

We have seen many cars these past few weeks, and not one can pull the train or even move on its own. They all need the big engine to lead the way. That big engine is not any good without an engineer to drive it. It takes both the power of the engine and the eyes of the engineer to make the train move. Without the engineer the engine is blind. In the Gospel today, Jesus asks, "Can a blind man lead a blind man?" Of course not. You need eyes to move around, whether you are a person or an engine. Jesus says, "Why do you call me 'Lord, Lord,' and not do what I tell you?" For an engine to move safely along the tracks it takes a lot of planning. At every crossroad there has to be a signal that blinks red lights and rings a warning when the train is coming. When the train gets near to the crossing, it blows its whistle or sounds its horn. That is to warn the people that the train is near and that they should pay attention. Every once in a while someone doesn't heed the warning and there is an accident. If you hear, why do you not obey? The warning at the railroad crossing is there to save your life. Hearing Jesus' words and obeying them is the way to save your life. Now you understand how important the engineer is to the train, how the cars cannot move without the power of the engine.

Now we come to the most important part of our train, and we haven't even mentioned it. Can you tell me what we forgot? The train track. That is what makes it possible for all the other things to work. The track is the guide for the engine and the whole train. If the track is laid on a solid foundation everything will run smoothly and safely. Every time there is a bad storm and the track is washed out, the train must come to a stop. All the power is useless because there is no track. Jesus talks about houses built on good foundations that stand when the floods come. This is the final message of our train series. It takes good track to show the way, that is the Bible. It takes power to make the train move the engine, that is God in our lives. It takes people with good eyes to help us see the dangers ahead, that is the engineer, our relatives, our teachers, and good friends. It takes cars to follow and do all the work. That is us. If we don't hear God's word and do it, if we don't see what has to be done and do it, God's good earth that he has given us just won't be worth living in. Let us make God's world work right, and each of us do our part.

The Transfiguration of Our Lord
(*Last Sunday after Epiphany*)

Gospel Lesson: Luke 9:28-36
Key Word: **Altered**
Objects: Two glasses of water; three bottles of food
        coloring

Our word for today is *altered*. That means "changed." That is what happened on Transfiguration Day. It means Jesus was changed. Before we talk about that, I think we will do some magic. We will make some changes right here, before your very eyes. Do not take your eyes from this great trick for one second or you may miss something.

I have two glasses of plain water. I need four volunteers to help me with this great trick. You will be amazed! You will be baffled! You might even say, "I didn't know the pastor was a magician." I want two of you to stand by this glass, and you two, stand by this one. Have I ever met any of you before? Say no, that is what a real magician does. Nice and loud, have we ever met before? (Kids holler, no) (Ask the first child) What is your favorite color? (Whisper, say yellow) See, with practically no help from me, he picked yellow. (Drop two drops of yellow food coloring into the water.) Did you see the change? Now the water is yellow. (Tell the other child to say his favorite color is orange.) (Add one drop of red food coloring into the yellow water.) There, you asked for orange, you have it. (Ask the third child his favorite color; say red.) There you have it. (Drop red food coloring into other glass of water.) Now, _____, your favorite color must be purple. (Add one drop of blue into red water.) You asked for purple, and there it is.

We saw change right here before our eyes. The clear water went from yellow to orange, and from red to purple. Thank you, boys and girls, for your help. A good magician needs good straight men, and you did a fine job. What we did here today, with a little food coloring, you can try at home. We were trying to show you change. In our lesson today, Jesus took Peter, James, and John up on a mountain to pray. Jesus often took his disciples to a quiet spot to pray and relax. What Peter, James, and John saw was really something more than what we saw with our water trick. Moses and Elijah had been dead for a long time, and suddenly they were standing with Jesus. They talked with him, and then they disappeared. Jesus seemed to glow pure white, and then a cloud came down and said, "This is my Son, my Chosen; listen to him!" Jesus changed back to the way he was, he looked the same. He was ready to go down the mountain and continue his work on earth. It is interesting that the little change we made was done with water and food coloring. The change in your life comes from a little water in your baptism. Change is a wonderful thing. As God's children we are changed people.

First Five Sundays of Lent

This is an interesting series that gives you two options on how you want to handle the children's participation. You can use the object of food as in the other series, or you can have the food brought in each week and let them "feed the hungry" as a Lenten contribution. I hope you will feed the hungry. If you do, it will take some advance promotion. You should publish a complete list of all the foods, in the parish paper, so parents can prepare. At least two additional lists in the Sunday bulletin, two weeks prior to the start of Lent. A weekly reminder in the bulletin for next week's contribution would also be helpful. Pick the charity you want to receive the food and you will be set. Leave the food in the altar area throughout the Lenten season for all to see.

Objects Required
- ☆ box of muffin mix
- ☆ can of chicken soup
- ☆ can of fruit
- ☆ can of beef stew
- ☆ box of cookies

First Sunday of Lent

Gospel Lesson: Luke 4:1-13
Key Word: **Temptation**
Object: A box of muffin mix

During Lent we will be talking about food. I think it would be a good idea if all the children would join me and bring in an item of food each week, so that we could be a part of giving someone who needs help a little something at Easter. I see some of you have been reading the notices about our children's sermon project. Great! Let me tell you how it will work. Each Sunday I will tell you what to bring in the next week. I am certain some of you may forget at times, but you can make up for it the next week. As we go through these five weeks, we will be able to give a poor family a good start on their Easter dinner. Do you all understand? Maybe your parents can remind you, a list on the refrigerator door might be helpful, also.

Our word today is right out of the Gospel lesson. It is *temptation.* Who knows what temptation means? When there is a dish of candy on the table, dinner time is near, and you have been told, "No candy before dinner." Then you are left alone. That is temptation. No one would ever know if you had one little piece. You are tempted, just as Jesus was. If you decide to have a piece of candy, you failed. You gave in to temptation. This was Jesus' trial. After forty days in prayer and fasting he was weak and very hungry. That devil is a pretty smart guy. He knew Jesus was hungry. He knew how weak he must be after such a long time without food. The first temptation was food. "Turn those stones to bread. You can do it; nothing to it," the devil said. Turning a stone into bread is a pretty good miracle. Those of you who brought in muffin mix today, hold it up. This is just a little miracle. Don't open the box, trust me. Inside is some powder, with a few lumps in it. It certainly doesn't look ready to eat. When your mother adds a few other things to it, like eggs and milk, and then bakes it, you have something very good to eat. A little miracle. This is our bread to feed the hungry. Jesus was tempted three times in the wilderness. He was weak from hunger and tired, but he held fast to what he believed. He did not accept the devil's offer to take a shortcut. He did it the hard way, he did it God's way. That is what we will be doing this Lenten season. The food you bring to the altar each Sunday will feed some families at Easter. A miracle happening right before your eyes, as the pile of food grows.

Don't forget the can of chicken soup next Sunday. If you forgot your muffin mix today, next week will be all right.

Second Sunday of Lent

Gospel Lesson: Luke 13:31-35
Key Word: **Brood**
Object: Can of chicken soup

O ur word today is a strange one. It is *brood*. This word is not used too often, at least I hardly ever hear it. What does it mean? In this case it means "to protect or cherish," or "to protect and love." If Jesus said to us right now, "I will protect and love you, you have nothing to worry about," we would go along with that. You just can't ask for more. The Pharisees came out to warn Jesus that Herod was going to kill him. You must remember that Jesus never did get along well with the Pharisees. Why would they come out and give him this warning about Herod? Herod was the ruler of Galilee, where Jesus was preaching. Herod did not really want to kill him, just scare Jesus away, get him out of his territory and bother someone else. That was the message Herod really wanted the Pharisees to tell Jesus. Jesus was not fooled by this phony message and said, "First I finish my task, then I will move along." Then he said something no one understood, later we all would understand what Jesus was saying. "It cannot be that a prophet should perish away from Jerusalem." This sounded strange to those who heard it. Who said anything about Jerusalem? Jesus knew Herod would not kill him until the time was right, and the place was right. That would be Good Friday in Jerusalem. Jesus always loved that holy city where the Temple was located. There were synagogues located all over the country, but only one Temple, the one in Jerusalem. The people of Jerusalem never really accepted Jesus, and only he knew that the next time he went there he would be put to death. Jesus preached one of his better children's sermons. I call it a good children's sermon because it tells a story with an illustration so simple everyone can understand. He uses the illustration of himself as the mother hen who gathers all her chicks under her wings, so that when you look at her sitting there, you would never guess she had her chicks hidden. That is how safe you would be. Totally hidden from all danger. That is what Jesus wanted to do for his beloved Jerusalem. The people said, no. This is also what he wants to do for us. Will we reject him? I hope not.

Last week we had our muffin mix that represented the bread. Today, just as Jesus said he would be the hen to help Jerusalem, we are going to help someone too. How many remembered your can of soup? Bring them up here and put them with our food from last week. The pile is growing. In a few weeks we will have many things and we can say, Have a nice Easter, to someone. All because of our children's sermons. Now don't forget next Sunday, a can of fruit, any kind of fruit.

Third Sunday of Lent

Gospel Lesson: Luke 13:1-9
Key Word: **Fruit**
Object: Can of fruit

Today is the children's sermon to end all children's sermons. I want you to make a note of this lesson, not the whole lesson just the thirteenth chapter of Luke, verses six through nine. You might want to memorize it, if not, keep it written on a piece of paper in your pocket so you can have it ready when you need it. We have a problem here. I wonder if you grown-ups could leave,

46

this is just between us kids. Never mind, you can stay. You will find out about this anyway. Let me tell you what this lesson says. It says, loud and clear, "give me one more chance." How about that? When you do something wrong and your mom or dad descends on you, and you know this is it, they are mad. You are in big trouble. Remember the great children's sermon and say Luke 13:6-9. That should stop them, just like when you hold a cross before a vampire. They will stop dead in their tracks.

A man had a fig tree in his vineyard. For three years he came to get some figs. Every year he was disappointed, there were no figs. Finally he told the man who cared for his vineyard to cut the tree down. He was tired of coming for figs and never getting any from the tree. The man who ran the vineyard said, "Let me see if I can give this tree some special attention. I think it will have figs by next year, if not, we can cut it down then." There it is, boys and girls, the Bible says, Give one more chance. Today we have something unusual in our sermon. Our word and object are the same; the word is *fruit,* and our object is a can of fruit. Our pile of food looks pretty good, the muffin mix, soup, and now fruit. We are beginning to get a nice meal together. We will feed many this Easter.

Our word for today is a different kind of fruit. This is often called the fruit of the spirit. The fruit of the spirit is love; doing good to your friends; feeding the hungry (we are doing that this year); helping and visiting the sick. The fruit of the spirit is all of the great things we should do because we are Christians. That is what the story in the Gospel talks about. If you are not a producing Christian, then you will be cut down. You bear fruit, or you take up space, be careful. God may get impatient with you.

One other thing, I almost forgot the first part of the Gospel lesson is the one your parents have to remember. When you do something bad, and they are angry with you, say Luke 13:6-9; then they will say Luke 13:3. Now you are in trouble. Luke 13:3 says, "Unless you repent, you will perish." *Repent* means "to feel sorry and seek forgiveness." Well, we had a good thing going for us for a little while, but I guess we lost again. You do not just keep on getting another chance, you have to ask forgiveness and feel sorry. Next time you are in trouble, try to repent, you might get to like it.

Next Sunday, we will use a can of beef stew.

Fourth Sunday of Lent

Gospel Lesson: Luke 15:1-3, 11-32
Key Word: **Scorecard**
Object: Can of beef stew

Our word today is not in the Gospel lesson, in fact, it is not even in the Bible. The word is *scorecard*. Everyone knows what a scorecard is. If we play a game of golf, baseball, or football, almost any game, someone has to keep score. It is the way we know who won and also when the game is over. This Gospel lesson has many people keeping score. The Pharisees and scribes were keeping score on how many times Jesus ate with sinners. That was a very important game for them. The prodigal son was keeping score on how much was due him, and then, how fast he could spend it once he had the money in his hands. The father was keeping score on his sons and how they were doing. The older brother was keeping a scorecard on how good he was, and how bad his younger brother was. You can't tell the players in this lesson without a scorecard.

Suppose your parents kept a scorecard on you. How well would you do? On the wall in the kitchen would hang a piece of paper with many squares on it. Maybe one hundred little squares. Every time you did something bad you would get a mark in a square. When all the squares are filled in, you are done. You have to move out, you are on your own. You have lost the right to be a member of your family. It doesn't matter if you are 6, 10, 14, or 20, when the scorecard is full, out you go. I wouldn't want to play in that game, would you? God keeps a scorecard on all of us, but he wipes it clean, and we can start over, if we ask him. Do you keep a scorecard on your friends? That can be a dangerous game.

Now, back to our three main players. The father gave his older son everything he would ever need in his whole life, most of all his love. He gave his younger son his freedom, even to go and do something dumb. Then he forgave his younger son when he came home again and asked to be forgiven. Remember last week we talked about the word *repent*? The young son came home sorry for what he had done and asked forgiveness. The father did forgive him. Now we come to the place where we all get in trouble. That younger brother took the money, had one long party until all his money was gone. Then the father said, "That is all right. I am just so happy you came home." He planned a big celebration in the son's honor. But to the older brother, enough is enough. "I have been here working twice as hard because that bum of a brother took off, and now you expect me to celebrate his homecoming. Not on your life. It just isn't fair." Love is never fair, but it is always forgiving. That is the real test for all of us. Can we accept what is right, even if it isn't fair?

Today they killed the fatted calf; that is the best piece of beef. Today we continue to feed the hungry with our cans of beef stew. We do have quite an assortment on our pile of food. This will be a great Easter for so many people, especially those of us who gave; it feels so good. Next week is the end of our meal. If we bring in a box of cookies, we will have a dessert.

Fifth Sunday of Lent

Gospel Lesson: John 12:1-8
Key Word: **Alone**
Object: Box of cookies

Jesus loved Bethany. When he was on the way to Jerusalem, whenever he could, he stopped there to spend the night. He had many friends who lived there, and he was always welcome. Today's stop in Bethany is a sad one for Jesus. In one week he would be crucified, his disciples would be scattered, hiding out, afraid for their lives. You can just imagine that as Jesus looked back on his three-year ministry, and looked ahead to the cross, he must have been very weary and discouraged. He looked at Lazarus and remembered the time when he had raised him from the dead. He surely felt that much had happened since then. He wondered if his disciples would be able to carry on the work that was started, after he was gone. Then Mary did something very nice for Jesus, and Judas, one of the disciples, started to gripe about wasting all that money on Jesus. The ointment was expensive and could have been sold and the money given to the poor. Jesus says, "Let her alone, let her keep it for the day of my burial." Not one of the disciples seemed to hear what he said. No one said, "For your burial! Are you going to die?" They just went on eating, all wrapped up in their own thoughts and problems. Our word for today is *alone*. Sometimes it is nice to be alone, other times it is just awful. This was one of those times when Jesus seems to be all alone in a room full of friends. None of them could feel what he was feeling. He knew that in a couple of days there would be a big parade for him, and he also knew that the happy time would not last very long. How can we cheer up Jesus? Let us do one of the things he asked us to do. Feed the hungry, bring comfort to those in need. That is what we have been doing these past five weeks in Lent. We have fruit to start our meal, chicken soup is the next course, and beef stew with muffins to go with it. Finally, cookies for dessert. Our pile of food looks ready to give to some needy family. Whenever God's people, especially children, reach out to help others, God smiles and thinks that someone is listening to him. We listened and we did something about it. I am proud of all of you who made this possible. Thank you. After all these weeks of talking about food, next Sunday our object will be a stone, but I will bring my own, you won't have to contribute.

Palm Sunday and Easter Day

These two Sundays work together. Palm Sunday is the talking stone; Easter Day is the stone that talked. You will need two stones. They should be at least six inches high and able to stand without any support. On Palm Sunday, place the stone at the appropriate time in the sermon, at a high spot. Perhaps on the side of the pulpit, or have a high stool nearby. You will have to look at that stone and talk to it. Try to convince the kids you really expect it to talk. That will be the secret of success. On Easter, introduce a new stone, but the one from last week is still there. Give it another chance to talk, then introduce the new one, this one can't miss, at the appropriate time.

Objects Required
☆ two large stones

Palm Sunday
(*Sunday of the Passion*)

Gospel Lesson: Luke 19:28-40
Key Word: **Silent**
Object: A stone

E very year we celebrate Palm Sunday. I think it is one of the
happiest days of the church year. We sing and talk about the
triumphal entry into Jerusalem that Jesus made. All the great
religious leaders of that day were greeted in the same way.
People put palm branches and cloaks on the road. This was to
show respect. The palms and coats also made a path that would
not permit the honored guest to set foot on the ground. The road
was to be completely covered. There were so many people
there, they had no trouble covering the ground with the palms
and coats. Everyone was happy and having a good time. Today,
the balloon man and the hot dog vender would also be there.
This was a very big parade. Did I say everybody was happy? I
spoke too soon. Let us look at the last few lines in the Gospel
lesson. There they are again, those old Pharisees. They seem to
follow Jesus everywhere. Not to hear what he has to say, but to
find fault with what he says. The crowd shouted, "Blessed is the
King, who comes in the name of the Lord!" If there was one
word that really made the Pharisees nervous, it was the word
"king." The church had a deal with Pilate. If they did not bother
Rome, Rome wouldn't bother them. The Pharisees were afraid
that somehow Rome would hear about Jesus being called king.
They warned Jesus, right in the middle of the parade. "Teacher,
tell your disciples to be quiet." The word for today is *silent.* There
are times when the worst sin of all is to be silent. It would have
been so easy for Jesus to say, "Don't call me king, it could get us in
a lot of trouble." Jesus would not allow his people to be silent.
This was the day for Jesus to be declared king. If that made the
Pharisees nervous, too bad, but they would not be silent.

Now, I have a treat for you. I told you our object this week
would be a stone. This is not just any old stone, boys and girls, it

is a talking stone. Let us see if we can get it to say something. Hello, stone. Hello, stone. (Hand stone to a child.) Hold this up to your ear, maybe it is whispering and I can't hear it. You can't hear anything either? I know what is wrong. This must be one of those stones that would cry out if Jesus told the crowd to stop calling him the king that comes in the name of the Lord. Here are all these people in our church, and in churches everywhere calling out, "Blessed is the King who comes in the name of the Lord!" Here it is two thousand years after Jesus told us about the talking stones, and we still celebrate the parade and the king. We still can't get our stone to talk, I am sorry, because so many of us are here today, our stone has nothing to cry out about. I hope people never forget who is the King, and that my talking stone never will have to cry out. (Take the stone.) Did you hear that? I think I heard the stone say, I hope I never have to cry out either. Hmmm!

Easter Day
(*The Resurrection of Our Lord*)

Gospel Lesson: Luke 24:1-12
Key Word: **Dawn**
Objects: Same stone from last week and a new stone

Happy Easter! This is a great day for those who believe in Jesus. Do you know that of all the religions in the world, there is only one that has a Savior who died and rose again? All the rest, when the person dies, he is dead. That is one reason today is such a happy one for us. It is our victory day. Here is the stone from last week. Do you have anything to say today? No, all right, I will put you over here and get another stone that has a message for us today.

The women went to the tomb on the first day of the week, that is Sunday. They went at early dawn, not just dawn, but early dawn. That is our word for today, *dawn*. Dawn is when the first light of day comes, even before the sun rises. The women came early because they were still afraid of the priests and Pharisees.

In those days, you found a nice spot on the side of a hill, dug a cave, and you had a tomb in which to bury the dead. A big stone was put in front of the tomb to protect your loved one. It would take many men to roll the stone away. Here is our stone, not so big as the one at the tomb, of course, but it has a message for us today. Do you know what the first announcement of Jesus' resurrection was? Not angels, nor the empty tomb. It was the stone rolled away. This stone is the one that made the first announcement. He is Risen! Our stone from last week let us down, not this one, however. It was a relative of this stone who first said, "He is Risen!" Stones may not talk, but they can send important messages. One that changed the world forever (hold up stone), He is Risen!

Second to Seventh Sunday of Easter

The Book of Books
vs.
A Book

During these coming weeks we will be using a different book each week. At the end of each sermon, we will end with a comparison of that book and the Bible. You will need the books listed below and a Bible each week.

Objects Required
* ☆ book of magic
* ☆ book about fishing
* ☆ math or arithmetic book
* ☆ a love story
* ☆ Sherlock Holmes novel
* ☆ a book of prayers

Second Sunday of Easter

Gospel Lesson: John 20:19-31
Key Word: **Shut**
Object: Book of magic

For these weeks of Easter, we will be looking at books. All kinds of books. One of the most important parts of your education is the ability to read. If you can read well, the job of learning is made so much easier. Learn to love to read. If you do, your whole school experience will be a good one. The joy of reading is a pleasure in itself.

Our word for today is *shut*. When a door is shut you cannot get into the room. You can open the door and enter, you could break the door down, but you cannot walk through a solid door. We are not talking about just anybody, we are talking about Jesus. You do remember that he healed the sick, made the blind to see, and even raised Lazarus from the grave. Don't mess around with Jesus. No little wooden door is going to stop him!

His disciples were still hiding from the priests and Pharisees. Jesus was dead. If they could kill Jesus they could kill his disciples also. They were scared and hiding from the whole world. Suddenly, Jesus appeared in front of the entire group. Talk about being afraid! Jesus said, "Peace be with you." Can't you just hear them saying, Wow! was I scared! When the disciples finally recovered and knew it was really Jesus, they were overjoyed. They no longer had to hide, they would be taken care of. Here is a book of magic. You know, there are many in this world who keep trying to tell us that Jesus was a great magician. The devil, when he tempted Jesus, said just that: Do some tricks for the people then they will believe. I am sure that at some time, we churchgoers have had our doubts and thought, if only there was some sign I could see to let me know that God is God. The difference between the tricks in this magic book and the stories in the Bible is that every trick in the magic book can be explained. This book (hold up Bible) says miracles, not magic. You can't explain miracles, they have not been explained in two thousand years. Sometimes I have my doubts.

Thomas took care of us on that score. Thomas doubted. He said, "I will not believe. Prove to me you are Jesus." Jesus did show Thomas proof, and then Thomas said, "My Lord and my God." We cannot see Jesus as Thomas did. "Blessed are those who have not seen and yet believe." That is you and me. This is not magic, it is miracles. You will not see, but you can believe. This is a book of magic; this one is a book of truth.

Third Sunday of Easter

Gospel Lesson: John 21:1-19
Key Word: **Cast**
Object: Book about fishing

There are no fish in the fountains in the center of a busy city. If you want to go fishing, you have to go to the ocean or to a lake. I think it is interesting that in order to fish you need to be quiet. Jesus chose a number of fishermen as his disciples, and I do not think it was just by accident either. When you fish, you are in a world of your own. As you throw out the line and reel it back in, you have time to think. How many of you have ever gone fishing? If you went fishing, it was probably with an older person, your dad or grandfather. Remember how exciting it was the first time you went fishing? You must have been told many times that you have to be quiet, if you expect to catch any fish. Unless you were very lucky, you had to cast your line out over and over, there just did not seem to be any fish in that water.

Our word for today is *cast*. It means "to throw." How many times did you cast your line before you finally had a fish bite? Talk about excited! When you finally feel that tug on the end of your line and you realize you have caught a fish, you are really excited. Half the fun of fishing is the long wait in between catches. That makes it so exciting. If you do not keep casting out your line, you will not catch a fish. If you are tired or bored, you are done for the day. If you keep casting, you will eventually catch something.

Jesus' disciples had gone back to Galilee to their homes after the Resurrection. They went out to fish, just as they had done before Jesus came along three years ago and said, "Follow me." They were fishing just to pass the time of day, their hearts were not in it. They did not recognize Jesus when he came walking down the beach. They told him they had not caught any fish. He said to try again, and they did. This time they caught 153 fish! What a lot of fish! As soon as they saw this big load of fish, they knew this man had to be Jesus. Peter jumped from the boat and walked through the water to get to Jesus, he was so excited.

This book about fishing will tell you everything you need to know about the sport of fishing. It is good sometimes if you do not know too much about a subject, like fishing, to get a book and read up on it. That way you know how to get started. The disciples did not need to read this fishing book, they came from families who had been fishermen for generations. When it came to Jesus, turning these simple fishermen into fishers of men, they had a lot to learn. Jesus had to teach them to keep casting, to not give up, or become discouraged. They had to learn it was much more dangerous to go fishing for men than for fish. Many of the disciples died at a young age because they went fishing for men. I hope all of you get a chance to go fishing someday soon. It is a lot of fun and very relaxing. I also hope that everyone in this church remembers that we are all fishermen for Jesus; we all have to be fishers of men. This is a book about fishing; this is a book about fishing for men.

Fourth Sunday of Easter

Gospel Lesson: John 10:22-30
Key Word: **Believe**
Object: Math or arithmetic book

This Gospel lesson begins by saying, "It was the feast of the dedication at Jerusalem." Does anyone know what the feast of dedication was? Every year about the time we celebrate Christmas, our Jewish friends celebrate Hanukkah. It is a celebration of the rededication of the Temple in Jerusalem that started 167 years before Jesus was born. The first celebration lasted eight days, and even today it lasts that long. The date of Hanukkah changes, but it is usually around the middle of December.

Jesus was in the Temple, and a number of the leaders of the Jews cornered him and said to him, "If you are the Christ, tell us plainly." This upset Jesus. He had spent a good part of his ministry healing the sick, raising the dead, preaching that he was the son of God, and still everywhere he went people still wanted to know if he was for real. Our word for today is *believe*. The way Jesus uses this word gives us a good idea that he was getting tired of answering the same old questions. He says, "I told you, and you do not believe."

You have to remember that a big business around Jerusalem was raising sheep. That is why when Jesus wanted to explain something, and wanted it clearly understood, he would use sheep as part of the illustration. Did someone ever accuse you of doing something that you did not do? The tough part about that is, there is no way for you to prove you did not do it, they will just have to believe you. The people keep saying, "We don't believe you." You can't prove anything, so all you can do is say it over and over again, then you finally get angry. That is where Jesus was, the only difference was he thought he had a good case to prove who he was by all the miracles he had performed. They still questioned him. Jesus said, "I am a shepherd. My sheep know me. You are not my sheep, if you do not know me. My sheep hear my voice, I know them, and they know me."

Let me tell you why I have chosen an arithmetic book today. In this book everything adds up just right. One plus one equals two, three plus three is six. Anything you find in this book adds up perfectly. In our Gospel lesson Jesus is trying to show the leaders of the Jews that he is the Christ. At the end of the lesson, he uses some math that probably confused the people more than it helped them to understand. Who, here, is good at arithmetic? The problem I want you to solve is addition. Who is good at addition? This will not be difficult, who wants to try? _____, stand up. The question is, how much is one and one?

59

Not too hard, is it? One and one is two? Wrong. Not according to the way Jesus does his addition. Jesus says, one and one is one. The people are so confused. They ask, "Are you the Christ?" He answers, "I and the father are one." Now, this is very simple. _____, stand up, please. You are one person. One person and one person, that is two. In our Gospel lesson, Jesus is introducing a new math. Jesus and God are one person. The arithmetic book cannot explain that, but the Bible makes it very clear. God and Jesus are one.

Fifth Sunday of Easter

Gospel Lesson: John 13:31-35
Key Word: **Glorify**
Object: Any love story book

This is the time when Jesus says good-bye to his beloved disciples. Jesus is ready to sum up his whole ministry and give final instructions to his disciples. Before he can do this he has one terrible job to get out of the way. If he is going to talk, he will have to be surrounded by all those whom he loves and who love him. There have been times when your mother has asked you to clean your room. You keep on playing and forget. When your mom shows up again and says, "I thought I asked you to clean your room," she is not angry, she sounds sad. She is disappointed that you forgot. You did not care enough to do the job right away. There seems to be a wall between the two of you now. You want to climb over the wall, but you don't know how. Then, you are asked again, and you jump right up and get busy. When the job is done, your mom says, "Thank you, you are a good child." The wall is down, you feel close to Mom again.

Jesus wanted to take this last chance to talk with his disciples, but there was one unfinished job he had to do first. Remember, Jesus had told Judas, "You are going to betray me. Go do it now." Our lesson starts as Judas gets up to leave to go betray Jesus to the priests. Once Judas had gone, Jesus was surrounded by those who love him. He wants to talk about the reason he is here on earth. First to *glorify* his Father. That is our word for today, it means "praise, honor, worship." That was the goal Jesus had set as he talked with his disciples, to praise, honor, and worship God. The next thing he wanted to tell them was his new law of love. Our book today is a love story. There are some rules to abide by when you write a love story. There must always be two people in love, it cannot be only one person. In the end of the story these two persons may not be living happily ever after. You can have a happy or an unhappy ending. There are sad and happy love stories. In some love stories, one of the persons even dies in the end. This is usually thought of as a sad love story. There can be many different endings to a love story.

Let us go back to Jesus. Judas is gone, and Jesus is telling his disciples the law of love that will be the sign of the church when he is gone. Peter is about to tell Jesus that if he is going, Peter is going with him. Jesus anticipates this and says, "Where I am going you cannot come." Here is the big difference between Jesus' version of a love story and this love story. In this story, two people, in love, keep telling each other how much they love each other. In the love story of Jesus, people keep showing others how much they love. Jesus tells us, if we love him, it will show. People will not have to ask, Are you a Christian? It will show. Not by looking at us, but by how we treat others, the things we do for one another, the love we have for one another. Here is one kind of love story, it does not show. The Bible is our love story. When people look at us, does it show?

Sixth Sunday of Easter

Gospel Lesson: John 14:23-29
Key Word: **Mystery**
Object: Sherlock Holmes novel

Most of us love a mystery story. The word *mystery* is our word for today. It is not in the Gospel reading, but Jesus sets up a mystery for the disciples. All of a sudden he is talking about a counselor, the Holy Spirit, who will come. What is he talking about anyway? Who is this counselor? Is this another man who will come down from heaven and take over Jesus' job when he goes to heaven to be with his Father? Who is this stranger who is suddenly introduced to the disciples? A mystery is something that is hidden or unknown. This is surely a mystery. Our book today is one in a series of mystery books. It was written by Sir Arthur Conan Doyle—a story of Sherlock Holmes and his friend Dr. Watson. In all the books, Dr. Watson is very smart; after all, he is a medical doctor. His main job is to help Sherlock Holmes solve the mysteries, but most important, he is to ask the right questions at the right time. Sherlock Holmes, taking a puff on his pipe, will say, "Elementary, my dear Watson." Then he will come out with a brilliant conclusion like, The butler did it. Then he proceeds to give an explanation of all the clues in the story, the ones Dr. Watson and we missed.

To be a real good mystery some people will be fooled, but someone has to come up with the answer in the end; or else the people are disappointed. We are surrounded by mysteries today; ones that do not have an end, but someday they will. Childhood diseases like measles, chickenpox, and polio were once mysteries, but no more, cures have been found, children no longer die from these diseases. The mystery has an end. Peter was like Dr. Watson, he always asked the questions. He was the first one to look for an answer to any question Jesus raised. Jesus knew how mysteries should go. He never started a mystery that did not have an ending. He also never made it easy for the disciples. They were put to a test before he gave them an answer. This time was no exception. He says, "I leave you my very special peace, not like any peace you have ever known. Do not worry, do not be afraid. I am going away, I will come again, and then you will have the answer to my mystery story." Not like this Sherlock Holmes mystery, "the butler did it," but the answer the Bible gives to the mystery that will come with a rush of wind on Pentecost, when the Holy Spirit came into the disciples and into each of us today.

Seventh Sunday of Easter

Gospel Lesson: John 17:20-26
Key Word: **Petition**
Object: A book of prayers

Our word today is *petition*. That is a formal request to one in authority. We have not had a Gospel like this for a long time. It is one of those Gospels that must confuse you young people, because when I have finished reading it, I have to read it again to see what it says. This is the last Sunday of Easter and the end of our series of books. It is my job to try to explain what this Gospel means. A petition is a prayer. Since God is the one in authority, all prayers are a petition. This prayer is separated into three parts. I do not know if you know that we all make petitions every day. We also separate our petitions into parts. You say to your mom, I want to go to my friend's house after dinner, and can I stay later than usual? Mom wants to know why. Here comes your petition to the one in authority in your life, your mom. All the kids are going to be there; petition number one. My friend has a new video game; petition number two. His mother will bring me home; petition number three. What you have listed are the reasons why you want to go to your friend's house, and why you should be allowed to go. That is a good petition.

Our book today is a book of prayers. It is a book full of petitions. How many times when we are in trouble do we say a little prayer: God help me out of this, or help me pass this test, and I will be the best kid ever. That is a prayer, and an appeal to one in authority. Let us return to our Gospel lesson to see what Jesus was saying in this prayer. First, we must know that this lesson is just the last part of the prayer that Jesus prayed. The first petition, verses one to five, was for himself. The second petition, verses six to nineteen, was for his disciples. The third petition, our lesson for today, was a prayer for the church. That is all of us. We are the church that Jesus prayed for so long ago. He asked God to look out for his disciples for all time, to let us

63

know that God loves us, just like he loved his son, Jesus. When we are in trouble, and we ask help of God, we have a right to make that petition. When you are worried about a test, you should study hard, but when you are ready to take that test you can say, Help me, God. In this prayer Jesus made arrangements for all time for you to go directly to the Father with your petitions. You think something like a test is silly to pray about? God is a very busy God. He can't take time to worry about you and your test. But he can, and he will. Jesus set it all up for us in this prayer. If you love him, and need him, call on him. He will always have time for you. Jesus died so that you could go directly to God with any problem. Try it, it works.

Our two final books agree. What is in this book of prayers is in this book, the Bible. There is no conflict this week. I think it is a nice way to end our book series, in agreement.

The First Eight Sundays
after Pentecost

Since Pentecost is a long season, it is split into several series. The first of which is eight weeks. The objects for this series are hats. (Trinity Sunday is not included.) Each week when it is time for the children's sermon, bring out your hat, and have a child to be your official hat wearer. Build up to the hard hat and make a big deal about your fantasy of wearing a hard hat. This series should be fun.

Objects Required
- ☆ Sunday school superintendent
- ☆ serviceman's hat
- ☆ woman's hat
- ☆ head scarf
- ☆ hard hat (construction worker's hat)
- ☆ man's hat
- ☆ policeperson's hat
- ☆ fireman's hat

The Holy Trinity
(First Sunday after Pentecost)

Gospel Lesson: John 16:12-15
Key Word: **Hear**
Object: Sunday school superintendent or a teacher

Today is Holy Trinity Sunday, the day we celebrate the God who is three in one: Father, Son, Holy Spirit. As I listened to the Gospel lesson with you, I thought the people who chose this lesson must have forgotten it is Trinity Sunday. Does this lesson have anything to do with three in one?

What a way to start the season of Pentecost! They are going to confuse us early, we still have twenty-six more Sundays to go.

We will not panic, however, let us take another look at the Gospel to see what we missed. We must have missed something. (Move your lips, but make no sound. Then ask, "Can you hear me?") Did you hear what I said? No? I cannot understand that. I thought I said it loud and clear. I will try again (this time aloud). "Can you hear me?" Now you heard me. Our word for today is *hear.* The first time I spoke you could not hear me, then I spoke again, and you could hear. First someone must speak, then someone must hear, and finally the people who hear must understand.

My object for today is a big one. I doubt that any one of you children could pick it up and bring it to me. Who thinks they are the strongest child in this whole room? All right, _____, you may get our object. I want you to go to Mrs., Mr., or Ms. So-and-So (name the Sunday school superintendent or the head teacher) and carry the person up here to me. That might be too much for you, so just lead that person by the hand. You can both stay right here. Why do you think I had _____ bring this person up here? This is our Sunday school superintendent. What does the superintendent of the Sunday school have to do with a Gospel lesson we do not understand? Let us ask this strong person first. Any idea? Anyone else? (Turn to the superintendent.) I hope I can remember why you are here or we are both in trouble.

This person is in charge of our Sunday school, from preschool class to the adult classes. If our preschool teacher was sick, the superintendent would probably say, That is no problem, we will just have her students sit in an adult class. Those youngsters would hear each word that the teacher said, but they would not understand anything, they are children and not able to understand an adult lesson. Remember, someone speaks, someone hears, someone understands. We have classes for different ages so that everyone can hear and understand.

Look what just happened to our Gospel lesson. Jesus said, "I have many things to say, but you cannot hear them." That does not mean they were not listening, it means they heard but could not understand. Make certain you are in the right class so you can hear and understand.

Jesus then says, "All that the Father has is mine."

It really is a Trinity lesson, the Father, the Son, and the Holy Spirit, speaking to every class in our Sunday school at a level that can be understood. Remember, hear what they have to say, that means to listen; then study and think about what you heard, so that you can understand the message for your life.

You can take the superintendent back now. Thank you.

Second Sunday after Pentecost

Gospel Lesson: Luke 7:1-10
Key Word: **Worthy**
Object: Serviceman's hat

Here we go again, another one of those Gospel lessons. We know we cannot work or earn our way to heaven. It is a free gift from God. That gift allows us to hope for heaven. Jesus is walking on a road going to a town called Capernaum. A Jewish man stopped him and said, "I am a very important person at the church in this town." He then told Jesus about a man, a Gentile who was a centurion (he commanded one hundred men), who had a servant whom he loved dearly. The servant was very sick and going to die. He wanted Jesus to help this man's servant. Jesus looked at the leader of the Jews and the look in his eyes must have said, How did you ever get involved with this hated Roman Gentile? The very man whom Rome sent to oppress my people.

At this point, the man saw the look in Jesus' eyes and tried to explain. "This man is worthy to have you help him, he built our synagogue." Jesus was interested in seeing what kind of a man was worthy. Do you know what *worthy* means? It is our word for today. It means "deserving." If you do your chores at home you deserve a treat, maybe cookies and milk. When your parents are very good at their jobs, they deserve a raise in pay. You always have to do something worthy to deserve something special. If someone stood up today and said, "I will give you all the money you need to build a new big church, I will pay all the bills." That man would deserve a special thank you from us.

Jesus wanted to see the centurion. He started to follow the Jewish man to the house of the Gentile, the soldier. Where is my soldier's hat? (Go to the closest boy and bring him up with you.) If we are going to see a centurion, I need a soldier with me. Jesus had walked a little way when he was met by messengers from the centurion. The messengers told Jesus that he did not have to go to the house. The centurion says, "You are a busy man. I am a soldier, I give orders all the time, when I say go, they go. I am not worthy to have you come to my house." Now we see what the problem was in the first place. The centurion did not say he deserved a favor from Jesus, it was his Jewish friends. The centurion said, "I am not worthy. I deserve nothing. Just say the word and my servant will be healed."

Jesus turned to his disciples and said, "I tell you not even in Israel have I found such faith." That explains why Jesus thought this man deserved a favor. The leaders of the church said to Jesus, "He is worthy, he built our church." Jesus healed the servant because the man showed so much faith; that is what made him worthy to Jesus. Now this proves what we said in the beginning, You cannot work your way to heaven. It is faith that makes you worthy, Jesus showed us that in this Gospel lesson. Thank you for your help, little soldier.

For the next few weeks we will be using many hats as our objects. If you want to wear one, just let me know, and you can join me.

Third Sunday after Pentecost

Gospel Lesson: Luke 7:11-17
Key Word: **Compassion**
Object: Woman's hat

L ast week we had one of the boys wear our soldier's hat. This week I need a young lady for this hat. (Put the hat on a girl.) Now remember, you are a widow whose son has just died, so be very serious, also hold on to your hat so it doesn't fall off.

Last week we had the servant who was so sick he was dying, and Jesus healed him. This week we have a man who is already dead, that has to be a much tougher challenge for Jesus. Why did Jesus heal the servant? Does anyone remember? It was the faith of the centurion. We said that is why Jesus works miracles, he does it after you show your faith, you are then worthy. This time it is all together different. The widow did not show great faith. No one came to Jesus and said this man had great faith. Jesus walked up to the dead man, who was the only son of this widow. He had compassion on the woman. That is our word for today, *compassion*. What does that word mean? "The feeling for another's sorrow or hardship that leads to help." I think before we go any further in this lesson we need some history.

Did you know in Jesus' day most people died before they were forty years old? One who lived to be fifty was very old; someone who was sixty was ancient. Today there are many people who live to be eighty or more. The next thing you need to know is that people had many children in Bible times. Many of these children died when they were quite young. Those who became young adults could work in the fields as farmers, or have a trade to help support their parents in their old age. If you did not have much money or many children, you were in trouble, if you lived to an old age.

The woman in this story was in good shape. She had lost her husband, but she had a son who supported her. The worst thing that could happen to her would be to lose her son. That is just what happened, he died. As Jesus walked down the road toward a little town, called Nain, he passed the funeral procession. He saw the poor widow, and he had compassion. He felt sorry for her, so he helped her. He said, "Do not weep." He turned to her dead son, and said, "Young man I say to you arise." Just that simple. He had compassion, he did not see great faith. This was the first time Jesus showed us that he was human as well as God. Remember our word from last week was *worthy,* meaning "deserving." We do not know whether this widow and her son were worthy, Jesus did not even seem to care. He felt sorry for them, and he helped. Now our widow here can have a smile on her face. Not only because her son was dead and is now alive, but because Jesus, who loves us and cares about us, and does good things for us understands how hard it is to be human. He feels sorry for us and reaches out to help. Not because we are worthy or deserving, but because he has compassion. He cares and he helps.

Fourth Sunday after Pentecost

Gospel Lesson: Luke 7:36–8:3
Key Word: **Listen**
Object: Head scarf

This lesson has many lessons. There are three that I want to tell you about today. Here is a scarf, will one of you girls come up and pretend to be a woman for the day? Do you know how to put this on? I hope so, I'm afraid I will not be much help. (After the scarf is in place) You were not one of the real nice ladies of the town. The Pharisees called you a sinner, so I guess you would be a bad lady. A Pharisee named Simon invited Jesus to his house for dinner. The practice in those days was to stretch out on a couch instead of sitting around a table. If you were an honored guest you were seated near the host. The servants washed your feet, the host kissed you to make you feel welcome, and then put some special oil on your forehead. Jesus was not the honored guest, so he was at the far end of the room. He received no fancy treatment. Simon, his host, did not have much respect for Jesus.

A lady crept into the room to see Jesus, and since he was near the door she had no trouble finding him. Simon did not like this at all. He was having a nice dinner party, and all of a sudden this lady is crying and making a scene; her tears running all over Jesus' feet, then drying the tears with her hair, and kissing his feet. Enough is enough. Simon got tired of this and said, "You are a prophet, you should know what kind of a woman this is."

Our first lesson—put Jesus at the honored spot in your life. The second lesson is, *listen* to what Jesus says. And this is our key word for today, so listen.

Two men owed a man some money. One owed him fifty dollars, the other five hundred. Neither one could pay him, so he said, "Forget it, I forgive both of you your debts." Which one of these men will love him more? Simon answered, the one who was forgiven more. Now Jesus has Simon set up, and he is about to teach him the third lesson for today. "You call this woman a sinner. She is doing more for me than you did as my host. If she is such a big sinner, just imagine how grateful she will be if I say to her, 'Your sins are forgiven.' " While some of the people said, Who does he think he is; Does he think he can forgive sins? Jesus paid no attention to them; he just looked that lady in the eye (take the girl by the hand) and said, "Your faith has saved you; go in peace."

Remember last week Jesus had compassion on the widow, it was not faith, but compassion. This week we are back to normal. First you show your faith, then Jesus will say, "You are forgiven." Give him top place in your life. Listen to the lessons he has to teach. Be ready to accept his forgiveness, after you show him that you love him.

Fifth Sunday after Pentecost

Gospel Lesson: Luke 9:18-24
Key Word: **Save**
Object: Hard hat

L ook at the hat I have for today! I always wanted one of these. When you walk past a big construction site, you will see a sign that reads, Hard Hat Area. What does that mean? Right, if you don't have one of these on your head, you cannot come in. That must be really great. When the boss comes to look at the job, he gets out of his car with his hard hat in his hands, puts it on, and walks right into the hard hat area. Do you know why you have to wear one of these at the site of a construction? If someone is working up high and drops something, and it hits you on the head, it doesn't hurt, it just bounces off. The hat may even save your life. I would really like to be the one to wear this hat, but there is someone else who wants to. (Have a child picked out.) Can I put it on for just a second, then you may have it? Thank you.

Do you get a feeling that today's children's sermon is about the pastor's fantasy? Wait until you see some of our other hats, I am sure one of them I will have to wear myself.

Are you wondering what the lesson for today had to do with a hard hat? Let me tell you our key word. It is *save*. Jesus talks about saving your life and losing it. Do you know what *save* means? It is "to keep safe from harm or danger." If all you try to do with your life is play it safe, to save it, you will never get a chance to live your life.

A year or so ago, a boy we knew only as David was born with a problem; his body could not fight off disease. If he was exposed to any germs he would get sick and probably die. The doctors put him in a special plastic bubble. Some of you may remember this brave boy; it is a true story. David lived in this plastic bubble for twelve years. He never touched his mother or father, or another living person, so he would stay germ free. Finally it was decided to try giving him a bone marrow transplant operation, to see if he could be helped. The doctors thought he might have a good chance to be normal, and his parents had to make a decision whether to have the operation or not. They finally asked David, "Do you want to take the chance?" Remember, he could go on living in his plastic bubble and save his life, or have the operation and take the chance that he would lose his life. David said he would take the chance. His bubble was keeping him alive, but that was not enough, he wanted to live too.

David had the operation, and two weeks later he died. David did not sit in his plastic bubble, with his hard hat on, playing it safe. He came out of his bubble, and took a chance on life. Jesus said, "Whoever would save his life, will lose it; and whoever loses his life for my sake, he will save it." Jesus does not want us to go into a hard hat area without a hat to show we are not afraid. Jesus does not want us to wear a hard hat for the rest of our lives, just to always be safe. Jesus took chances to show us the way to live. We must take chances to live his way. Before you go, let me try the hard hat one more time. How do I look? Thank you.

Sixth Sunday after Pentecost

Gospel Lesson: Luke 9:51-62
Key Words: **Bad day**
Object: Man's hat

D o you ever get up in the morning and think to yourself, This is going to be a bad day? Sometimes you can just feel it. Our words for today are *bad day*. The females in the congregation today can sit back and relax. Today it was a man who gave Jesus a bad day. Here is a man's hat. Will some boy come up here and let me borrow his head for a while? Thank you. Put this on, and get ready, because we are going to pick on you this morning.

The end of Jesus' earthly ministry was near. He was headed for Jerusalem. The shortest way was through the Samaritan lands and cities. Jews and Samaritans were not friendly, they had been enemies for years. Jesus decided to stay in this Samaritan town for the night and to preach. He sent a few disciples ahead to make the arrangements. When they came back they reported that they did not want Jesus to come to their town, or to preach. When James and John heard this they became very angry. They told Jesus they wanted to destroy the town: We do not have to put up with these kinds of insults from the Samaritans. Jesus told them to calm themselves, they would just move on to the next town. That was the first thing to happen to Jesus to make this a bad day. Someone said, Do not come, you are not welcome. (Look at the boy in the man's hat.) Jesus and the disciples walked on down the road. A man came up to Jesus and said, "I will follow you wherever you go." Jesus could tell this man wanted something in return for following him, and he said, "You get nothing if you follow me, not even a bed at night." The man left. That was the second thing that made this a bad day. (Look at the boy with the hat again.) Another man came up to Jesus and Jesus said, "Follow me." The man said, "Wait until my father dies, it would break his heart." One of the oldest excuses in the world. Another person, for the third time, had given Jesus a bad day. (Look at the boy with the hat again.) This day was getting worse all the time. Another man said, "I will follow you, Lord." But first he had to go home to say good-bye to his family. This man, although he told Jesus he was ready to follow him, wanted some time to think it over before he made his final decision. This was the fourth man to make Jesus have a bad day. (Look at the boy with the hat.)

I knew of a boy, only fourteen years old, an Orthodox Jew, who was converted to Christianity. When he went home to tell his father, he was turned out of the house, late at night, and told, You are dead. This boy was ready to follow Jesus even though he was only fourteen years old. He gave up everything to follow Jesus. Later in life, he became a minister and was responsible for leading many Jewish people to accept Christ. He was not like the man who just could not make up his mind. (Go over to the boy and say) You have been a good sport to allow us to blame Jesus' bad day on you. Thank you very much for your help.

One other thing before we end today's bad day. Let us go back to the start of this bad day. Remember, James and John wanted to destroy the town? That was just the first of four things that happened to Jesus on this bad day, but he was never angry, never discouraged; he just went right on telling everyone he met the good news. Learn from Jesus. We have a message to deliver. Stay calm. God will be with you and help you always, especially during the bad days that come.

Seventh Sunday after Pentecost

Gospel Lesson: Luke 10:1-12, 17-20
Key Word: **Subject**
Object: Policeperson's hat

O h, wait until you see our hat for today! It is a policeperson's hat. I think we have had too many boys up here the last few weeks, so this week we are going to call one of the girls to come and be our policeperson. Isn't it great that every day new jobs are open to women? By the time you young people are ready to pick a career there will be nothing impossible for girls to do. So, now we have our policeperson.

As you read the Gospel for today, you may wonder why we have a policeperson. I will try to explain by telling you what our key word is; it is *subject*. "Lord, even the demons are subject to us in your name." What do you think the word *subject* means in that statement? It means "bringing under some power or influence, conquering." That is what makes the whole U.S.A. work. Did you know that? We are subject to laws. We must obey these laws. Sometimes we forget, and that is when a policeperson comes and tells you, "Now you have to pay for not being subject to the law."

Let me explain how we are a nation of laws. When you go for a ride in your car, and you come to a stop sign, you must stop. The driver never says, "Is there a policeperson around? If not we won't bother to stop." It is the law, so we stop. These laws that make our city or town work, come from God. It is the result of God making his law and giving us guidelines for our laws. Remember last Sunday, James and John were angry at a town and tried to have Jesus destroy the town; they had had enough

75

insults. Jesus was very gentle and said, No, let us find another town. This week he has chosen seventy persons to go out to other places to prepare the way for his visits. He tells them to go boldly, not as beggars. These seventy were going out with power. Today, when we send missionaries all over the world, one thing we almost always do is send doctors to start hospitals. We do just as Jesus instructed the seventy, "Heal the sick and say to them the kingdom of God has come near you." The seventy worked hard and followed Jesus' instructions.

Finally, on the day for them to return and report to Jesus, it says, "They returned with joy." They came back to tell Jesus, "It worked." They had gone into the fields to harvest for Jesus and it worked. They obeyed the laws that Jesus had given them. Just like the stop sign, there is not a policeperson at each stop sign, people stop because they know it works that way. The seventy set a new standard that missionaries still follow today, "Heal the sick." Be subject to the law, it works. Thank you, police person.

Eighth Sunday after Pentecost

Gospel Lesson: Luke 10:25-37
Key Words: **Went to him**
Object: Fire fighter's hat

Remember when we had a hard hat a few weeks ago, and I told you I always wanted to wear one? I also said a hat would come along that I could not resist. Here it is—sorry kids, this one is mine. Can you guess what kind of hat this is? A fire fighter's hat! Let me show you how I look in it. Ever since I was small I wanted to be a fire fighter, and now I have my chance. (Put on hat.) Well, I guess I better give up my dream, and my hat also. Who wants to be a fire fighter today? (Put hat on person.) You look good in it too.Now, why do we have a this hat today? The lesson was the great story of the good Samaritan. Most fire departments have two jobs to do. One is to put out fires. What is the other? In many towns they run the rescue service or ambulance. If you are hurt or there is an automobile accident, the rescue truck comes rushing in to help care for the injured.

Back to the Gospel lesson. A man was on the road from Jerusalem to Jericho; there are only eighteen miles between those two cities. The road went right through the mountains. Do you remember how in the movies of the Old West, the bad guys always hid in the mountains and jumped out from behind a big rock to attack the good guys? That is exactly how it was on this road. The bad ones robbed the poor man and beat him.

Our story tells us three men came past this poor injured man. The first was a priest, he was a very good man, but too busy to get involved. He was like a fire fighter who would just sit at home when the siren went off because he did not feel like helping anyone that day. He thought maybe someone else would do it. Then a Levite came by, he worked in the Temple too. He just walked on by, he did not seem to care. The Levite would have made a bad fire fighter. Now, here comes our kind of man—the Samaritan. A few weeks ago we learned that the Jews and Samaritans hated each other. Jesus picks a Samaritan as the hero, the good fire fighter in our story, in order to say, There is good in all of us. Do not judge people; try to love them. The good Samaritan heard the fire siren, and he was ready to answer the call. He *went to him*—our words for today. He stopped, helped, and made certain he would be taken care of until he was well. That is a good fire fighter.

When Jesus tells a story, he does not do it just to entertain. He does it to teach a lesson. To the lawyer, not an ordinary lawyer, but a man expert in Jewish law who knew all the answers, Jesus said, "We had three men, two of whom I am sure you respect, and one bad man whom you despise. The bad man turned out to be the good Samaritan. Which of these was a good neighbor?" The lawyer answered, "The one who showed mercy." Jesus told that lawyer, two thousand years ago, and is saying to us today, "Go and do the same." Be a good fire fighter, be ready whenever you are needed. Help your neighbor. May I have my hat again? (Put on hat.) I do think I look good in this.

This is the last of our hat series. Next week we will look at magazines.

The Ninth to Twentieth Sunday after Pentecost

This is a series on magazines. Often there will be two magazines to use as a comparison. It is a long but interesting series. There may be a chance you could be on vacation for part of this time. If your supply does not use a children's sermon, it is possible to pick up the series when you return, with no problems. Enjoy your vacation knowing the interruption will not even be noticed. If the supply has used the series, fine, no interruption.

Objects Required
* ☆ religious magazine and *Good Housekeeping*
* ☆ daily devotional booklet
* ☆ *Better Homes and Gardens*
* ☆ *Sports Illustrated*
* ☆ comic book and *National Geographic*
* ☆ *Popular Mechanics* magazine
* ☆ *Bride* magazine
* ☆ *Money* magazine
* ☆ bicycle magazine
* ☆ movie magazine
* ☆ *House Beautiful*
* ☆ seed catalog

Ninth Sunday after Pentecost

Gospel Lesson: Luke 10:38-42
Key Word: **Serve**
Objects: Religious magazine and
    Good Housekeeping

For the next few weeks all our objects will be magazines, different kinds of magazines. To get us started, today we will use two magazines. But we will come to them later.

I am the pastor, but I could never get away with this in my house. Let me see if I can set up the Gospel lesson like it happened at Martha and Mary's house in Bethany. We will pretend this happened at your house. You are going to have company for dinner. Someone very special. Your mother has spent many hours cleaning the house, and it looks very nice. She has planned a nice dinner: roast beef, mashed potatoes and peas, rolls, cole slaw, and chocolate sundae. You know a big dinner like that takes a lot of time to put together. There is cooking to be done, setting the table, making sure everything is perfect and that the beef is not overdone. Your mother has asked you to help her, so that everything will be ready and perfect.

The man who is coming for dinner arrives, he is greeted at the door by your mother, and she tells him to sit down, dinner will be ready in a little while. He should read some magazines until dinner is on the table. She goes back to the kitchen and expects her helper to follow. You do not come to help, and there is much to be done. She goes back to the living room, and you are sitting on the floor listening to stories the guest is telling. Your mother, a wee bit annoyed, tells the guest that he should wait until they are all at the table to tell his stories, and she needs her helper in the kitchen so the dinner can get on the table before the meat is ruined. The guest agrees that Mother has been busy getting the meal ready and that is necessary, but says that she should leave the helper alone, that you have chosen the good job to do. Now, boys and girls, how would that go over in your house? My wife would not like that one bit.

Now, let me show you our two magazines, and see if we can find what Jesus tells us in this lesson. Here is a religious magazine, and here is a copy of *Good Housekeeping.* Martha, we called her the mother, gets *Good Housekeeping,* Mary gets the religious one. This Gospel lesson follows the story of the good Samaritan. Remember the lesson of the good Samaritan was being a good neighbor. Today Jesus is teaching us how important it is to serve not only your neighbor but to serve God. That is our word for today, *serve.* The job Martha did in cleaning the house and making the dinner was very important. There is more to serving Jesus than worldly things. You have to stop, sit at his feet, and learn the lessons he has to teach. Jesus loved both Martha and Mary. Martha did not think what she was doing was important. Jesus thought it was just as important as Mary learning at his feet. Jesus loves us all, he thinks whatever we do to serve him is important. Sometimes it is good housekeeping and sometimes a religious thing. You serve God in your heart and with your hands. Serving God in any way is what is important.

Tenth Sunday after Pentecost

Gospel Lesson: Luke 11:1-13
Key Word: **Ask**
Object: Daily devotional booklet

What do you love more than anything in the whole world? (You will get many answers—my mom, my cat, my bicycle. You will probably be very surprised at some of the strange answers, just smile along with the rest of the congregation.) Some of you parents may be surprised that you were not number one on the list. Don't worry, as the children get older you may move down the list, but eventually we all make a comeback to the top. Let me tell you why we are talking about what you love the most. In the Gospel today the disciples ask Jesus to teach them a prayer. Did you notice it is almost like the

Lord's Prayer that we use here in church? This is Luke's version, a little shorter. The Lord's Prayer we use is from Matthew (6:9-13); it is longer, but says the same thing. In this prayer Jesus teaches us one of the big lessons we have to learn. All you have to do is ask. That is our word for today, *ask*. Do you know what "ask" means? It is important that we know just what Jesus means when he says ask. It means "to request by words." That is exactly what prayer is, isn't it? In the Lord's Prayer Jesus says you should ask for God's kingdom to come. Then ask for yourself; first for food, then forgiveness. The last thing to ask for is to give us strength in time of trial or temptation. Just ask, that is how much God loves you. When your puppy is hungry, you feed him, because you love him. That is what we are talking about, love. You love that puppy and take care of him. How about God? He loves you, and he will take care of you, just ask.

I have been talking about how we talk to God. Often the Gospel lessons are an ongoing story, just like a book. Each chapter leads into the next. The good Samaritan taught us to love our neighbor as we love ourselves. Martha and Mary taught us loving God was as important as serving people. This week we learn that God loves us more than anyone in this world. He loves us so much, if you were the only person in the world, and he had to die on the cross to save only one, he would, for you. Just ask, he will help you.

Have you heard the mealtime prayer, "Come Lord Jesus, be our guest, and let these gifts to us be blest?" That little prayer, many of us know, has taught us how to pray. Jesus' disciples wanted the same thing—teach us to pray. Jesus gave them the Lord's Prayer, which is often called the perfect prayer. I am sure you all have a best friend. You talk to this person almost every day, you see each other at school and play, and if you do not see your friend, you call on the telephone. That is how best friends are. God is our best friend, we should talk to him each day. Do you have trouble talking to God? Need some help? Our magazine is a devotional booklet. This is a way for you to talk to God each day. Here is how you could do it, you are never too young or old to start. Have your parents read it to you. Take this booklet home, and use it every day. Just ask, he is ready to give.

Eleventh Sunday after Pentecost

Gospel Lesson: Luke 12:13-21
Key Word: **Covetousness**
Object: *Better Homes and Gardens* magazine

Our word for today is a big one. The word is *covetousness*. Do you have any idea what it means? (I am sure none of the children will know, if one does happen to come up with the right answer, praise him.) I will tell you. Covetousness is when you desire possessions. There is something you want so much, you do not know how you can live without it, you would do anything to get it. What do you want more than anything? A new bike, a new game, a video cassette, your own television set? We could probably think of one hundred items we would like to possess. These things are for me, just for me. I want it to be mine. Is it wrong to want something so much? Let us say that the other night, when your mother was making dinner, something happened to the oven. She became angry and said, "This oven never works. I want a new one." Is that what Jesus says in this Gospel is a sin? Poor Mom, if that is true, all the moms in the world are in trouble. Suppose you read in the newspaper tonight that you can win a bike if you become a newsboy, and you want a bike, so you take the job. Then in six months you win the bike because you worked so hard, is that a sin because you wanted that bike so much? I hope not.

What does Jesus mean when this brother in the Gospel lesson asks for what is his? He was left all this money by his father. All the young man wants is what is left to him. His older brother will not give him his half, so he asks Jesus, "Tell my brother to give me my half." Jesus sides with the older brother. He says, "I am no judge." Then he tells the story of the very rich man who had everything he would ever need, but he was not satisfied. He wanted more. He built more barns, and soon had more than he could use. He was finally satisfied. He sat down and said, "I have more than I will ever need, now I can relax and enjoy life." God said to him, "You fool." That night the man died. What good did all that he had do him? He forgot God. Why did Jesus get so upset with this young man who just wanted what was his? The answer is in today's lesson. Where is our magazine? Here it is, *Better Homes and Gardens*. Here are the nicest things, even new ovens for that mother who wanted one. You can really become excited about a magazine like this. Is this wrong?

Jesus knew what the Jewish law said. When a father died, all his goods were left to his children equally. The oldest son controlled all the money and land and paid out the profits to the rest of the family. The young son wanted his all at once. Then Jesus said, God knows what you need. It will come to you as you have need of it. You cannot demand that God give you everything at once. You children get almost everything you need from your parents. They know what you need and what is good for you. God knows what we all need and when. It will come to us when God is ready and when we are ready to accept it.

Twelfth Sunday after Pentecost

Gospel Lesson: Luke 12:32-40
Key Word: **Girded**
Object: *Sports Illustrated*

Today we are going to talk about our word and our magazine, then we will go on to the Gospel lesson and the other stories. Our key word is *girded*. This is an old word. It is used over and over in the stories in the Bible. Verse thirty-five is an interesting verse that has a lot of familiar words, so let us take a close look at them. "Let your loins be girded [that is our word], and your lamps burning." In the pictures we see of Jesus and the men of his time, they all wore gowns. They were like dresses, going almost to the ground. Where is my magazine? It is *Sports Illustrated*. What does *Sports Illustrated* have to do with this lesson? In a football game, when the referee blows the whistle to start the game, you had better be dressed and ready to play. In track, when the starter fires the gun, you had better be in the starting blocks, in your track suit, ready to run. In all sports and games we play, you have to be ready or you will be left behind. The officials will not wait for you. That is what *Sports Illustrated* is all about. It reports who was ready and who won. There is not much written about who lost or wasn't ready to play.

Let us go back to our key word and verse, "Let your loins be girded." If I ask you to sit and guard my house, and you have on a big, flowing robe, and you had to move quickly, you would probably fall on your face. Gird your loins means just to put on a belt, so you can be ready to move quickly and won't trip over your clothes. The last part of that verse says, "Keep your lamps burning." If you will be guarding my house at night, you will need a light. Keep your lamp burning. Watching a house can be pretty boring. Often when the owner came home, he found his watchman asleep. The reason it was important to have a guard who stayed alert was because all the houses were built of clay. A robber did not have to go through a window or door, he would dig a hole through the side of the house and not be noticed. Jesus tells us that the master went to a wedding. The weddings lasted a day or two, sometimes a whole week. This was the best time for a robber to do his work.

We have talked about *Sports Illustrated*, football, running races, putting on your belt, and keeping your lamp ready. All these things were about being ready. What is Jesus trying to tell us? He is trying to tell us to be ready to meet him. We will meet him some day. He may come back while you are still alive. Will you be ready? When you die, you will meet Jesus, and he will be ready for you. We have to be certain we are ready to meet him. We never know when it will be, but it will happen. Stay alert, keep your lamp burning. Get in the starting blocks; be ready for the kickoff; ready, set, go.

Thirteenth Sunday after Pentecost

Gospel Lesson: Luke 12:49-56
Key Word: **Choose**
Objects: Comic book and *National Geographic*

Did you hear that Gospel lesson? I am supposed to have a children's sermon based on that. Maybe I should have taken a vacation day and let someone else work this one out. If I understood the Gospel lesson, Jesus came to bring strife, division, and families fighting. If that is not enough, he also came to cast fire on the earth. How do you like that? Doesn't it sound like a fun type of God to worship? Let us try to find some way to explain this so children can understand it.

Remember we are using magazines in this series. Today we have two magazines, a comic book and a copy of the *National Geographic*. We all know the comic book is going to be fun. (Pick a boy.) If I asked you which of these magazines you would choose, which would it be? *Choose* is our word for today. (The boy probably picks the comic book. Select a girl.) You do not get to choose since there is only one left. Come up and hold this for me. If you would have had a chance to choose, which one would you have chosen? Our word is not in the lesson. I had two magazines, a comic book and a *National Geographic*, I asked _____ to choose one and he took _____. A comic book is fun, and there is nothing wrong with having fun. The *National Geographic* can be fun too, but its real purpose is educational. Even a little thing like deciding what magazine to read means making a choice. Do you understand that now? All through life we have to choose. Jesus is talking to a crowd of people. They are all relaxed, enjoying what Jesus is telling them. Blessed are the peacemakers, the persecuted, the meek. These are from the Sermon on the Mount. The people were getting the idea that following Jesus was going to be fun, like a comic book. Just relax and enjoy, Jesus will do it all. Jesus decides it is time to give them a little *National Geographic* treatment; time for some education.

What Jesus says is a look into the future. When he says, "I have a baptism to be baptized with," he is talking about Good Friday and dying on the cross. Then he talks about father against son, mother against daughter, and all the rest of it. Jesus is not saying I came to break up families. He is saying you will have to choose. If you choose to follow me, it will not be easy. Your mother or father and friends may not want to follow me. You must choose, them or me. My way is a way of peace, but if it is necessary to choose, you choose me, no matter what it costs you.

This little passage from Luke does not change the Sermon on the Mount or the other things Jesus said about love and peace to all people. It does say, It will not be easy, be ready, someday you may have to choose.

Fourteenth Sunday after Pentecost

Gospel Lesson: Luke 13:22-30
Key Word: **Shut**
Object: *Popular Mechanics* magazine

Have you ever been playing at night, when it was almost bedtime, and your mom or dad called and said, "Put your things away, it is time for bed"? You were right in the middle of something that was really fun, so you kept right on playing, figuring they didn't mean right now, only when you were ready. Then this voice calls again, "Are you getting ready for bed, are your things away?" You decide that if they knew how much fun you were having, they wouldn't make you stop. Then, "I mean now!" There is that tone of voice that means, Next time I will come in there and then you will wish you had listened. Wow! You should see how fast things are put away now. Toys in their places, your teeth brushed, clothes off, and into bed in a big hurry. You all know that special voice that says, "I mean now."

Our key word for today is *shut*. Let me show you what that means. I need someone to help me. When your mom says, I have a surprise for you, shut your eyes, you know how to shut them so

87

they are not quite shut. Watch. Shut your eyes so they look shut, but so you can see a little. Now, how many fingers do I have here? (Hold up two.) Right, two fingers. Your eyes looked shut, but they were not. Now shut them tightly. Squeeze them shut. That is what "shut" means, "to close tightly." You can shut a door. If you want to come in all you do is turn the knob, and the door will open. If you shut it tightly, you lock it so you cannot get in. You are locked out. If you do not know how to shut your door so no one can enter, you need a magazine like this one. It tells how to do all those little jobs around the house, and how to put on fool-proof locks so no one can get into the house once you shut your door.

I think it is about time we take a look at our Gospel lesson to see what all this is about shut eyes and shut doors. Remember someone asked Jesus how many people will be saved and go to heaven with him? Jesus is not too encouraging. It seems to me that his answer is not too many. Jesus says, It is not easy. People hear me tell stories, and they like my stories. I sit down to eat and people come to eat with me. They hear me pray and they say, That was nice. People ask, Do you believe in Jesus? Everyone in this church will answer yes, we love Jesus, but when Jesus says, "Show me by the way you live," we fail. It is just like what we talked about when you were asked to put away your things. You did not listen until you heard that tone of voice that meant now. Jesus says, "The door is open, it is a narrow door, come on in." He has invited us over and over again. In this Gospel lesson he finally gets that tone in his voice that means, Now. You must do it now, before the door shuts, so you cannot open it anymore. Jesus is inviting us again today, "Come on in, I love you." Are you going to ignore that word until he finally gets that tone and says, Now? I would not take a chance, when you finally decide, the door may be shut. What a shame you did not listen and answer when you had a chance.

Fifteenth Sunday after Pentecost

Gospel Lesson: Luke 14:1, 7-14
Key Word: **Marriage**
Object: *Bride* magazine

Today we are going to a wedding. Have any of you ever been to a wedding? They are a lot of fun. I have another question. Have any of you been in a wedding? I know a lot of you older people have, but I just want to hear from the kids now. Anyone been a ring bearer or a flower girl? In case you do not know, the ring bearer has a pillow on which the rings are placed, and he carries them to the minister who will be performing the wedding. The flower girl carries a basket of flowers, and she comes down the aisle before the bride. Let me tell you a secret. If we have a wedding with a ring bearer and a flower girl, I never have to guess who the parents are. All I do is stand here and look out at the congregation, and I will see a couple with big smiles on their faces, and then I will hear a sigh of relief as their children do their job well. Those two children have the best seats in the church to see the wedding.

Our key word is *marriage*. That is what happens at a wedding, people get married. Usually when there is a wedding they have ushers, all dressed up, who will take you to your seat. The family sits on the front row, in the place of honor. All the relatives sit in the second row, and then come friends behind them. Let me show you our magazine for today—*Bride* magazine. It tells you all about weddings, what to do and what not to do. What is right and what is wrong. If you are invited to a wedding of someone you work with, you better take a seat at the back of the church. If you walk in and take a seat in the first row, the bride's family's place, an usher will probably come up and say, "Excuse me, this row is reserved for the bride's family." You will have to move, and it is most embarrassing.

In the Gospel for today, Jesus is talking about two things. First he talks about where to sit at a wedding. Who would have thought that *Bride* magazine would have something in common with the Bible? In Jesus' day, it was not always relatives who had the best seats, but also the richest and most powerful men in town. Most men knew where to sit; they knew exactly where they rated at a feast and took their seats with no problem. What Jesus is saying is, How great an opinion do you have of yourself? If you think you are a big shot, then you go and take the seat next to the host. You may be asked to give up your seat and move down a little. If you take the worst seat the host will say, "Come up here closer to me." That would be quite an honor. Jesus teaches us a lesson, one he uses over and over again. "He who exalts himself will be humbled, he who humbles himself will be exalted."

The second lesson of this Gospel is: if you want to have some fun, have a party. Feed your friends, that is fine. It will not only be fun, but if you are lucky, you may be invited to the next party your friends have. Then you will be even. Jesus' kind of party would invite all the poor people who are hungry and really need the food you will serve. This kind of party is the kind Jesus wants us to give because the people cannot repay you with a party of their own. Jesus serves us, we cannot pay him back. We serve people, they cannot pay us back. Jesus sits and smiles, just like the proud parents—they are my kids, they did it right.

Sixteenth Sunday after Pentecost

Gospel Lesson: Luke 14:25-33
Key Word: **Cost**
Object: *Money* magazine

Today I have a magazine I am sure you boys and girls read from cover to cover each time you can get your hands on one. It is called *Money* magazine. I think I sense some disappointment in the faces of our kids. You don't read *Money* magazine? You should! When you have a dime, and you go to the candy store, how can you decide what is the best buy unless you have read this magazine? I hope your folks read a magazine

90

like this to help them with their money. We need good stewards in this church.

I haven't done too well with my magazine so far, let me try again. The word for today is *cost*. That is what this Gospel is all about. That is what life is all about, you have to learn to count the cost. Let us go back to the dime you had. Remember you were going into the candy store to see what a dime would buy (hold up a dime). I have an idea! Instead of going to the candy store to buy candy, which will soon be gone, I think we should go down the street and buy a new bike. You heard me, I will take my dime to the bicycle shop and buy a brand new bike (hold up dime). What kind of a bike do you think I can get for a dime? A bike would cost more than a dime, but maybe your mother would give you another dime, then with two dimes you would have plenty of money. No? I guess I had better sit down and find out how much a bike costs before I get my heart set on buying a new bike. I must say I am a little disappointed.

Let us go back to our Gospel lesson for last week and then for today. Last week it was all about parties and weddings, remember? This week Luke follows that kind of happy story with this one to remind us that if we want to follow Jesus, it always costs something. Jesus tells us, Do not just say you love me, and think that is all there is to it. I really wanted that new bike, but I did not plan too well; I only had one dime. Jesus tells us two stories today. First, a man wanted to build a big, beautiful house, with a pool out back and a big deck, so he could have his friends visit in the summer. He told all his friends about it, invited them to the housewarming party. He called a man in to dig the hole for the foundation. A mason came and put in a fine strong foundation. Suddenly, the man had no more money, only a dime. Just like buying a bike for a dime, he couldn't finish his house with only a dime. He forgot to count the cost.

The next story is about two kings. They each have an army. One has ten thousand men, the other has twenty thousand men. If I were the king with only ten thousand men what would I do? Talk things over with the other king. Right! The other king has twice as many men, he could wipe me out, the cost is too high, I think we should talk it over instead of fighting. Jesus said that to us, clearly, in this Gospel. The only thing that does not cost is his love for us. "If you want to follow me, because I love you, that may cost." Your family and friends may object. Sit down and make up your mind what is most important to you, family or Jesus. I am sure you children will not lose your families because you choose to follow Jesus. Someday, somehow, there may be a cost. Don't be surprised. Jesus told you, Everything costs if it is worthwhile.

Seventeenth Sunday after Pentecost

Gospel Lesson: Luke 15:1-10
Key Word: **Rejoice**
Object: Bicycle magazine

Our word today is *rejoice*. A pretty simple word. It is used in the Gospel today three times. Who can tell me what the word *rejoice* means? "To be happy or glad." When I listen to this lesson I always wonder what you think when you hear this story. When I was your age, and if I had ten coins I would have gone to the store and exchanged those coins for candy, or maybe a comic book. I could never save money. I hope you children can. Then there is another story about the lost sheep. Did anyone lose a sheep this week? Have you ever lost a sheep? Sometimes young people have trouble understanding some of the great Bible stories because we live in different times.

Let me show you our magazine for today. It is a magazine all about bicycles. How many of you have bicycles? I had a two-wheel bicycle, and I loved that bike. It wasn't a new one, it was pretty well beat up, but it was mine. How about a friend? Do you have a best friend? We have something in common, we each had a bike and a best friend. I had two good friends. We went everywhere together. We rode our bikes to school and we would lock them up to the bike stand with a chain. One of my friends had a lock and chain also; but the other, who had a really old bike, a real mess, would never lock his. He always would say, "Who would want that old thing?" One day, when we came out of school, his bike was gone. We could not believe it. Who would do such a thing? Now we had three good friends, two riding their bikes, and one running alongside. When he got tired, we had to stop while he rested or sometimes we rode on and waited for him to catch up later. It almost broke up our friendship. We always looked for his bike. Each time someone with a beat-up bike came along we checked the bike out to make certain it was not my friend's bike. My story does not end like the sheep and coin stories. After a few months of running, our friend finally got a new bike for his birthday. It came with a lock and chain.

Let me tell you what this lost bike has to do with our lesson. Each of us has lost something that we liked very much. It may have been something little. We told our mom about it, and she said, "Don't worry, it was just a little thing, you have others." It had nothing to do with the value of what was lost. Sometimes parents do not understand these things. That is the story of the sheep and the coin. It was not that ninety-nine sheep were not enough, the shepherd loved all his sheep, he wanted to find that one he loved. The woman who lost her coin wanted to find it, because she needed it. Just like the bike, it was loved and needed. That is the story of our Gospel lesson. Jesus is saying, "You are my sheep, I love you, and if you are lost I will search until I find you. If you are lost like the coin, I will look for you, because I need you." If you are lost, Jesus will not wait until you find your way back, he will find you. You know how you look for your lost toy? Just imagine how Jesus loves his favorite lost child. That may be you. He will find you.

Eighteenth Sunday after Pentecost

Gospel Lesson: Luke 16:1-13
Key Word: **Shrewdness**
Object: Movie magazine

I love this kind of Gospel lesson. God seems to be saying, "You did a good job," to all the wrong people. It is like a mystery story until we get to the end, and if we are lucky it will all be clear, and you will understand. Our word today is *shrewdness*. A big word, not used too often. Does anyone know what it means? It means "sharp, quick-witted, clever." In this story we assume that it is God who is the rich man, and he who says to the bad steward, You are very shrewd.

Let us get our magazine for today. It is a movie magazine. Shall we try to see what a movie magazine has to do with the unfaithful steward? First, a steward is one who is trusted to handle all the money, land, and people that a rich man owns. We have stewards today but they are called presidents of banks. The president is the steward of the money people place in his bank. We may even call them pastors. The pastor is responsible for the congregation that God has trusted him with. We may even call them Mom and Dad. They are trusted, by God, with you and your life to see that you grow in God's way. You are a steward also. You may get an allowance, you have to handle it well, and the other things that are yours; you are the steward of your possessions.

Now what does this magazine have to do with the story? Do you like mystery movies? I do. The kind I like best is the one that after a few minutes you can figure out who did the crime. Then, ten minutes later, you change your mind, because of some clues, and now you are certain you know the ending. Just when you sit back and say, This mystery is easy, I know who did it, you find you are wrong again. At the very end of the movie, when you find out who really did it, you usually say, "I knew it all the time." In our Gospel mystery story, God finds his steward is not honest, so he fires him. Then the shrewd steward decides he will give away more of God's money and oil and wheat so he will have some friends when he loses his job. That is bad. When God finds out our mystery story will come to an end. God will not put up with that. He fired this man, and now here he is giving away more of God's things. God says, "That was shrewd." This lesson and this mystery movie are not coming out as expected. The next twist in our mystery is, God did not say to the bad steward, You did the right thing. He said he was shrewd. The steward never told God he was sorry. He lived for money. His answer when he was in trouble was to think, How can I use God's money to get

94

myself out of this trouble? God said, Let him live in this world, he is shrewd and clever enough to make it.

Then we have a surprise ending. God says to us, "If I can not trust you with the things I give you, do you think I can trust you with heaven?" Money is not everything. It is how you use money that makes the difference. If you have a few toys, and your friend has many, but he breaks them as fast as he gets them, you have more than your friend. You have shown God you can be trusted. Choose God, or choose money. You can have both, you cannot worship both. Choose God and be a good steward.

Nineteenth Sunday after Pentecost

Gospel Lesson: Luke 16:19-31
Key Words: **Good—Evil**
Object: *House Beautiful* magazine

Last week we talked about the bad steward. The man God trusted with his money, and the man did not spend it wisely. You remember that God took the man's job away. This week Jesus tells another story with the same idea. It has a mystery too, let us see how it turns out.

There is a rich man, Jesus does not tell us his name, just a rich man. In front of this man's gate was an old, poor, sick man named Lazarus. The rich man had everything a man could ever want: a big house, many servants, a garden where he kept his expensive dogs. He loved his dogs. He also loved to eat. He had a big appetite. If I tell the adults how well he ate I could get in trouble. If I say he ate steak, lamb chops, veal cutlet, and beef Wellington, they would say, Now that's eating! You kids would probably say, That doesn't sound too great to me. But if I told you this man ate hot dogs, hamburgers, and hoagies, you would think that was great and your parents would think it was awful. We will just say he ate really good food. When he finished eating, the scraps were gathered together and the dogs would be fed. He does not sound like a bad man, he liked to live and eat well. He could afford it, why not? Our magazine is called *House*

Beautiful. A magazine that has lovely homes and gardens, even swimming pools. If you want to live like the people in this magazine it looks like you would have to be rich. I almost forgot poor old Lazarus. The rich man did forget Lazarus. All he wanted was some of the scraps that were fed to the dogs. He never expected to be invited inside the house for dinner. "No, Mr. Rich Man, do not invite me in, just throw me some scraps so I do not starve to death. If I do not get some food soon, I will die." The rich man went on feeding his dogs, and Lazarus did die. Want to see Lazarus' magazine? (Hold up empty hand.) He did not have money to buy a magazine. He did not even have an address to send a magazine to him.

God gave the rich man all his wealth and his life. That rich man enjoyed his money and his life. Do you think he owed Lazarus something to eat? In our world today, there are rich people and poor people; rich countries and poor countries. The rich man did not use his money wisely, he was a bad steward. God gave America great wealth, are we good stewards? We have two words today, they are *good* and *evil.* God is not against people who have money. All he wants is for you to be a good person with it, not evil. The rich man did not care if Lazarus lived or died, that made him an evil man. When the rich man died he went to Hades, he could not see Lazarus in heaven. Now it was too late for the rich man. He saw all his relatives and friends back on earth, and he tried to make a deal. Send someone back from the dead, then my friends, and all the people on earth will believe. God did just that. He sent his son, he lived with us, he died, he came back from the dead. Did Jesus convince you that he loves you? Do we all spend our time and money God's way? We have to answer that for ourselves. What is your answer?

Twentieth Sunday after Pentecost

Gospel Lesson: Luke 17:5-10
Key Word: **Faith**
Object: Seed catalog

Our word today is *faith*. I find it hard to believe that with all the words we have used, this is the first time we are using "faith." A part of this lesson is about faith. The disciples said to Jesus, "Increase our faith." I think that is a strange request for the disciples to make to Jesus, after all they had been through together. Let me try to explain why I think it was a strange thing to say. Have you ever tried to hit a baseball? Have you ever tried to run a race and win? Or to cook something? Have you tried to ride a two-wheel bike? If you want to do any of these things, what is the thing you must do before you try? (Get some answers from the children.) Let me tell you the most important thing you have to do first. You have to believe you can do it. Everything you try in life, you have to believe you can do it.

This is our last magazine in this series. I felt I could take some liberty on this last day. This is not really a magazine, it is a seed catalog. We have been talking about believing, that means "having faith." A seed catalog is the greatest illustration of faith you can find. I want you to look at the pictures in this catalog, and you will know what I mean when I say you have to believe. (Open the catalog to a beautiful display of flowers, and show it around.) If I ordered some seeds from this catalog, and bought ten pots and some soil, then asked ten adults to plant a seed and tell me what they expected to happen, I know that they would probably say: "I have been through this many times myself." "Mine never look like the pictures." "I do not have a green thumb." "Most of the time my plants die." Now I will give ten children a pot and some seeds, hold up the picture of the flower in front of them, and every one of the children will believe that they will get exactly what is in that picture. You know what? They probably will. That is believing.

The second part of the Gospel ties in very well with faith. It is

97

about being humble. If you believe that God can do anything and everything in your life, then you just have to be humble. How long has it been since your mom made a special dinner, one of your favorites, and when it was over you said to the rest of your family, "I think Mom deserves a standing ovation for that dinner"? All the family stands and claps for dear Mom. Your mother would like that, but she would not expect it all the time. She has a job and she does it because she loves you, and that is one way she can show it. Dad does not expect the family to be waiting at the door when he comes in from work, giving him cheers for going to work. We each do our job and serve each other because we love each other. We are all servants to one another and that means that none of the servants is greater than the other. We serve and we believe, that is the message today.

Twenty-first to Twenty-sixth Sunday after Pentecost

This is a short series in which we will use things found on your breakfast table. The series is flexible and can last for two Sundays or up to six, depending on how the church year works out this particular year. This is an easygoing end-of-the-year series.

Objects Required
☆ saltshaker
☆ knife
☆ napkin
☆ plate
☆ coffee cup
☆ spoon

Christ the King
(Last Sunday after Pentecost)

This is a one-Sunday sermon to wrap up the year. We will use a birthday gift to show the children that we look at the same thing in different ways, depending on our ages.

Object Required
☆ a wrapped birthday gift

Twenty-first Sunday after Pentecost

Gospel Lesson: Luke 17:11-19
Key Word: **Where**
Object: Saltshaker

Today we start a new series of objects for our lessons. From now until Christ the King Sunday, which ends Pentecost, we will be using things that we use every day. Not fancy items. In fact, if you had time for breakfast before you came to church today, you may have used our object or at least you may have seen it on the table. What we will be using for the next few weeks will be objects you see every day on the table where you eat. Today our object is salt. This is my saltshaker, right from our table at home. (Hold up shaker.) Salt is an amazing substance. I can put a little on my eggs in the morning, and the eggs will taste better. It brings out the flavor in foods we eat. There is a funny thing about salt. If you had some meat or fish that you wanted to keep, in days gone by, before refrigeration, you could put lots of salt on the meat and it would last a long time. When you were ready to eat it, the salt would be washed off and the meat would still be good to eat. A little salty maybe, but if you were hungry, like Daniel Boone, it was good, and it kept you alive. A little bit gives a good flavor; a lot will preserve food.

In the Gospel lesson today, Jesus is headed for Jerusalem, this may have been his last journey, we are not certain. Jesus went to Jerusalem many times to celebrate the holy days in the Temple. By law, the lepers could not come close to the road. Their disease was very contagious. So they stood back and cried out, "Jesus, Master, have mercy on us." We do not know whether these people believed or not, but Jesus gave them a test of faith. Remember, we talked about that before; first you show faith, then Jesus heals. The ten lepers were not healed immediately. Jesus said, "Go show yourselves to the priests." Let me explain the proof of faith. The priests in the Jewish nation had many jobs. One was that of a health officer. His job was to tell you what you could eat, how to kill it, and how to prepare it so you would not get sick.

100

When you suspected that you had leprosy, you had to go to the priest. He looked you over and told you whether you had it or not. If you did, you could not go closer than twenty paces to a clean person. If the clean person approached you, you had to call out, "Unclean, unclean." What a terrible way to live. Jesus said to the ten, "Go and show yourselves to the priests, show them you are clean." They looked at themselves and the leper sores were still there. In order to be healed, they had to start to go to the priests. If they had enough faith to take those first steps toward the priests, they would be healed. The ten left, and only one returned to Jesus. He came back to thank Jesus. He wasn't even a Jew, he was another good Samaritan. Our word today is *where*. Where are the other nine? Ten were cured, only one returned. This made Jesus very sad. Only one came back to say thank you. Every day Jesus takes care of you, he cares for you. Are you the one who says, Thank you, or are you one of the nine who forgot? Salt adds flavor and preserves. So does Jesus. He will add flavor to your life, and if you show your faith, he will preserve you forever.

Twenty-second Sunday after Pentecost

Gospel Lesson: Luke 18:1-8
Key Word: **Vindicate**
Object: A knife

This Gospel lesson tells us about a lady who was a pest. She had bothered this poor man day and night. Everytime he turned around, there she was saying, "Vindicate me." If you kids were the judge, you would have to run home and ask your parents what *vindicate* means. Do any of you know what *vindicate* means? It means "to give her what is rightfully hers." *Vindicate* is our word for today. We are not certain what it is she wants, or what she thought was rightfully hers. That is not important to our story. What is important is that she thought someone "had done her wrong." She wanted justice from this judge. The judge thought she was a real pest, but he was no prize either.

Jesus tells us that the man did not judge by God's laws or man's laws. He made decisions as he felt. This is not to say he was a bad judge, but judges were to follow Jewish law and be fair to all people. I guess Jesus knew this judge made some bad decisions. Let us see how fairly he settles this case. While I was buttering my toast this morning, I was thinking about the justice this man could hand out. Suddenly I realized, he could cut her loose. Just take his knife of justice, and by the power vested in him say, "Lady, right or wrong, you win. Go away and leave me alone." That is not very good justice. He cut her loose, he solved his problem, but we will never know whether this woman was really right or wrong. She was so persistent she wore the old judge down. Some of you may have had someone who pestered you until you were so sick and tired of hearing them whine all the time that you gave up and gave in. I guess I feel a little bit sorry for the judge. A bad judge and a pesky lady. I hope this story has a happy ending. All we have to do to find the happy ending is to go back to the lesson. "Pray and do not lose heart; will not God vindicate his elect who cry to him day and night." It is plain and simple. If you pray to God, day and night, he will give you what is rightfully yours. You are one of the elect, one of his chosen people. Pray a lot, be a pest. God loves it, and he will not desert you or forget you. He is a just God. His decisions are always fair. Trust God the judge.

Twenty-third Sunday after Pentecost

Gospel Lesson: Luke 18:9-14
Key Word: **Merciful**
Object: A napkin

Did you listen to the Gospel lesson today? I hope you did because by now you know our children's sermons are based on those lessons. Jesus is picking on the poor old Pharisees again. He always seems to be doing that. I think we should stop and see what it is about the Pharisees that upsets Jesus so much. The Pharisees had a special job in the life of the Temple and in the lives of the Jewish people. It was their job to see to the laws of the Jewish people. As the Jewish people wandered all over the land, with no homes and a different religion in each country, pressure was put on them by the local people to worship their way. They said that it did not matter anymore, God had deserted them long ago. As they wandered about, it was the job of the Pharisees to read the law to the chosen people, to bring them back on the path God had chosen for them as a test for his people.

In that time the Pharisees did a good job of keeping the Jewish nation together. They had a Temple in Jerusalem, part of the fulfillment of God's promise to his people. The Jewish people had a nation of their own, free to worship as they pleased. What do the Pharisees do now? Now we come to the reason, after the history lesson. The Pharisees forgot about love, compassion, justice, mercy, and forgiveness. This is the law, if you live up to the laws, you are perfect, like the Pharisees, God will love you and save you. Jesus said, "I have a new law, love one another." The Pharisees said, "Nonsense, the law will save you, not love." There it is—the Pharisees live by law, Jesus by love. What do you think was on my breakfast table that had to do with this lesson? A napkin. The Pharisees were trying to clean with a napkin to cover their sins and doubts. It is all artificial. It gets dirty, you throw it in the wash, or if it is paper, in the trash. That napkin will keep you from getting dirty while you eat, but it will not keep you clean forever.

Now let us look at the Gospel. Compare two men. One, the Pharisee, who thought he was perfect. Then the hated tax collector. The tax collector was even afraid to look up to heaven. He kept his head down and said a perfect prayer, "God be merciful to me a sinner." Our word today is *merciful*. The tax collector asked God to be merciful, that means "give kindness," more than I deserve or justice requires. The Pharisee was proud and perfect and wanted all to know it, even God. The tax collector was humble. He knew he was not worthy of God's love or forgiveness unless God would be merciful to him. You can use a napkin to keep the crumbs off your lap, but not to make you clean. Do not be proud, like a Pharisee, be humble like the tax collector, and ask God to be merciful to you, a sinner. He will answer your prayer.

Twenty-fourth Sunday after Pentecost

Gospel Lesson: Luke 19:1-10
Key Word: **Murmurs**
Object: A plate

A sycamore tree? I started thinking about Zacchaeus climbing a sycamore tree. I read the lesson many times and wondered what is a sycamore tree? If they are around here, I do not remember seeing any. What is a sycamore tree? We will have a botany lesson, because this is what I found out: It is "a fig tree growing in Egypt or Syria as a shade tree bearing a large fruit, good to eat." It is a member of the maple family. So, after all this time, we know what a sycamore tree is. Zacchaeus was a small man. We have no idea how small, but he must have been very short. He heard Jesus was coming, and he wanted to see this man so many people were talking about. He was a busy man—the head clerk of all the tax and customs people in Jericho, a big city in Jordan. As the caravans would come through Jericho, Zacchaeus and his assistant would stop them and collect a customs tax that would be sent to Rome. The taxes supported the army that was keeping the Jewish people in captivity. No wonder no one liked poor Zacchaeus. He worked for the enemy.

The people who knew Jesus was coming came out early so they could see him. Zacchaeus was so busy he arrived late. He could not see through the crowds, but he heard their *murmurs*. That is our word for today. The crowd was murmuring that Jesus was coming. Zacchaeus must have jumped up and down, trying to see. That was no good. Suddenly he spotted a sycamore tree ahead of where Jesus was coming. He raced to the tree and climbed up. Its branches reached over the street, and all of a sudden, he had the best seat of all. He just watched as Jesus approached. When Jesus was almost under the tree, he looked up and said, "Zacchaeus, come down, I am going to your house tonight." In this part of the world, if you ever had a holy man come to visit you, your house was blessed forever. Zacchaeus was so excited. How many times have we said it? Jesus did it again. He did not stay with the high priests or Pharisees, he picked the chief hated tax collector. No wonder people were murmuring. They said, "He is going to stay with that man. Does he know who he is?" Jesus knew what he was doing. He went to the house of Zacchaeus and had dinner.

Here is a dinner plate, not from the house of Zacchaeus, but from my house. It was at dinner that Jesus talked to Zacchaeus. Jewish law stated that if you took too much tax from someone, you must give it back and pay a fine or penalty. You must add one-fifth more to it, to make it just. Zacchaeus was a sinner in the eyes of all who knew him. He was a tax collector. Jesus asked him what he was going to do. He wanted to see some change in him. Zacchaeus said, "I will repay anyone I have harmed. Not one-fifth more, but four times more. I am a rich man, I will give half of all I own to the poor." That was good—sharing God's gifts with God's people. Zacchaeus passed the test. Jesus gave Zacchaeus the greatest gift of all. "Today salvation has come to this house," Jesus said. That is why we are here today, to hear Jesus say to us, "Today salvation has come to this house."

Twenty-fifth Sunday after Pentecost

Gospel Lesson: Luke 20:27-38
Key Word: **Sadducees**
Object: A coffee cup

Did you ever ask your mother a question and she said, Go ask your father? That is how I feel about this lesson, go ask your father, and then I will sit down. It is a tough one. Let us start by finding out who these three men were who asked the question. The *Sadducees,* our word for today, were leaders in the council of the Jews. They were the practical thinkers. They liked to reason things out. If you want reason then you will have trouble with the Resurrection. These men came to Jesus with a very serious question; they also were trying to trap him.

In Jewish law, when a man married and died before his wife had any children, she had to marry his next youngest brother. When they had children, the children would be considered the dead brother's. What the Sadducees wanted to know was, what if she married brother number two, and they had no children so she kept on marrying brothers three, four, five, and six, since there were no children and each of the men had died, what happens at Resurrection? Whose wife will she be? Can't you just see all the Sadducees sitting back, looking at each other and saying, "Let's see him get out of this one"?

I would like to show you our object for today—a coffee cup. You may not understand what a coffee cup has to do with this problem, so I will explain a secret I use, and I am certain your parents or relatives use also. In the morning, we older people are not too sharp. Often, at breakfast you will ask a question and take us by surprise. We don't know how to answer so we say, "Wait until I get a cup of coffee. Then I will answer your question." We are stalling. We need time to think. Now, about that question from the Sadducees. What was it? Whose wife will she be after marrying all those brothers? Since these men are scholars of the Old Testament, Jesus decides to quote Moses, one of the greats of the Old Testament. "Moses showed, in the passage about the burning bush, where he calls the Lord, the God of Abraham and the God of Isaac, and the God of Jacob, now God is not God of the dead, but of the living; for all live to him." Pretty clever. Moses talks about God and these three dead prophets as if they were alive. Jesus says not in body, but in the spirit. So he says to the Sadducees, Here is the answer, not my answer, but from Moses. Do not argue with me, argue with Moses. So which of the many brothers was with the woman in heaven? All of them. Not as people as we are here today, but as spirits forever, because in heaven there is no death. That was very complicated. I hope you could follow. Before you ask any questions I think I will go get another cup of coffee.

Twenty-sixth Sunday after Pentecost

Gospel Lesson: Luke 21:5-19
Key Words: **Endurance** and **patience**
Object: A spoon

E very time I read this Gospel lesson I think, *I hope I don't have to go through all that before I die. Maybe I will be dead and gone before this happens.* Before we all get depressed and leave the church, let us put all this in perspective. First, let me tell you who Jesus said this to and when. Jesus was sitting with some of his disciples—Peter, James, John, and Andrew—at the Mount of Olives, a little park that looked down on the Temple at Jerusalem. They were talking, and since Jesus knew he would die soon, he thought they should be told. It would not be easy for them when he was gone.

How many of you have ever done something dumb? Imagine that you were asked to push a button and dinner would start; it would be ready when everyone got home. You arrived home from school, just to drop off your books and then go to a friend's house to play, but first you must push that button. So you rush in, put your books away, change your clothes, and head for your friend's house. You have a good time, and now you must leave. Your mom is waiting at the door for you, but before you see her, you remember, the button. You forgot. You say to yourself, *I wish I were dead.* Then you get the old, I only asked you to do one thing. Everyone is mad at you. Dinner will be really late. Your father works hard all day, do you think he wants to wait for dinner? By now you stop wishing you were dead and wish you had never been born.

What Jesus is saying to his disciples is the same thing you must remember. Our two key words are *endurance* and *patience.* From

107

the time you are born until you are old and ready to die, you will always need these two things, endurance and patience. That means that whatever is happening, you will live through it. If I am patient, all this will change. I know, at the moment, your mother thinks you committed the biggest sin a child can commit. You forgot to push the button. Even this crisis will pass.

I looked at the breakfast table today, trying to figure out what item you can use from the beginning to the end of a meal. Anybody guess? It is a spoon. From breakfast cereal and grapefruit to the end of the day's meals, your spoon is working. It starts and ends the meal with you. Jesus is talking to his disciples, but he is giving us the same message. When I go away, things will not be easy. Let me give you Jesus' message for when life gets tough, or you forget to push a button—endurance and patience; soon it all will pass.

Next Sunday is Christ the King Sunday. The end of the church year. This is the last Sunday our object is something found on the breakfast table.

Christ the King Sunday
(*Last Sunday after Pentecost*)

Gospel Lesson: John 12:9-19
Key Word: **Raised**
Object: A wrapped birthday gift

Today is Christ the King Sunday—a day set aside to honor Christ as King of the world. This is also the last Sunday of the church year. The new church year does not start on January 1, which is New Year's Day, it starts on the first Sunday in Advent—next Sunday.

Today, the Gospel from John is the story of Palm Sunday. Do you think this is a strange time to have a Palm Sunday lesson? The story of Palm Sunday is in the other Gospels, but only John ties it in with the story of Lazarus being raised from the dead. That is our key word, *raised*. You remember the story of Palm

Sunday when people put palms and cloaks on the road for Jesus to ride on. Did you ever wonder how those people knew Jesus would be riding to Jerusalem on that road? Were posters put up saying, Jesus Is Coming? Were ads run in the newspapers? Only John tells us why this big crowd was waiting for Jesus and why they wanted to make him king. Only royalty received such a welcome.

According to John, the people had heard about Jesus raising Lazarus from the dead. They thought that maybe he would be bringing Lazarus with him. What an exciting thought. First the one who performed the miracle and then the one who was raised from the dead.

This should have been the happiest day in Jesus' life. After trying to get people to listen to him, they wanted to make him king. What a day! The crowd did not know who Jesus was, only that he had raised a man from the dead. The disciples thought this was great also. Now they would get some respect. Only Jesus knew what was really happening. Only he knew it would not be a happy occasion. He was fulfilling the Old Testament prophecy, "Behold your king is coming." That great day would end in Jesus' death. Our key word again, he would be *raised* from the dead.

We all have times when everyone around us is happy, but something is bothering us and making us sad. I have our object right here, a birthday gift for someone. Birthdays are fun and funny. When you are young and have a birthday, it is just great. Every young person I know wants to be older. Can't wait to go to school, then on to high school and college. Young people always want to be older so they can do something else. Then we have older people who do not want to have any more birthdays. Each birthday means they are getting older, and that makes them sad. They think about the good old days, when they were young. To young people you say, "Happy Birthday," they say, "thanks." When you say it to older people, sometimes they answer, "I stopped counting." All the crowd was shouting Hosanna, everyone was happy, but Jesus was counting. Soon his time of trial would come. Soon he would be King indeed.